PRESSED FLOWERS

THROUGH THE SEASONS

Margaret Kennedy Scott & Mary Beazley

✱

B T Batsford Ltd · London

ACKNOWLEDGMENT
The authors wish to thank the owners of some
beautiful gardens in Suffolk and Hertfordshire which
they visited while writing this book: Mrs H. Bain,
Mrs N. Gregory, Mrs M. Hole, Mr and Mrs D.
Liggatt, Miss C. Roberts, Mr and Mrs T. Rochford
and Mr and Mrs F. Webster. They would also like to
thank Julyan Rawlings for his photographs. The line
illustrations were drawn by Margaret Kennedy Scott.

By the same authors:
Making Pressed Flower Pictures (Batsford, 1979)

First published 1983
© Margaret Kennedy Scott & Mary Beazley 1983

ISBN 0 7134 4039 2

Filmset by Servis Filmsetting Ltd, Manchester
Printed in Great Britain by
The Anchor Press Ltd, Tiptree, Essex
for the publishers,
B T Batsford Ltd,
4 Fitzhardinge Street,
London, W1H 0AH

Contents

Introduction

This book is about preparing and pressing wild and garden flowers in the spring, the summer and autumn and the winter and finally creating with them flower arrangements that recall the special flavours of each season. Every one of the four quarters of the year has its own particular attraction, an identity which is recognised by the senses and is not dependent solely on whether the days are hot or cold. The common flowers which liberally decorate each season become part of this identity in our minds so that to many people 'daffodils and spring' are as synonymous as 'chrysanthemums and autumn'.

We have been pressing flowers for many years and have both found extra pleasure in creating designs with them that recapture a particular time of year. You have only got to glance at the picture in this book of poppies and grasses to think of summer sunshine and cornfields, while the black, white and sepia effect of one winter design directs us straight to the bare bones of January.

But if we are going to serenade the spring by making the pictures with only the early flowers, we shall have to decide when winter ends and spring begins before we can start picking.

How can we divide the year fairly into four acceptable seasons when there are some 600 miles between the north coast of Scotland and the Isle of Wight? The warmth of the first spring day in the south may be delayed for weeks before it creeps over the border and at the other end of the year the first snowfall of winter arrives in the Grampians while southerners are still sweeping up the autumn leaves in their shirt sleeves. The climatic differences between Cornwall and East Anglia too are very wide indeed, and even in one area the arrival of any season may fluctuate greatly from year to year.

If there is little to assist us from the national weather pattern in assessing where to draw the lines across the calendar, there is a great deal of accepted botanical and gardening lore which may give us guidance. Books on British flora covering both wild and cultivated plants have established categories of *spring*, as opposed to *summer*, flowers. Despite everything the tulip, as well as the bog-asphodel, has been pigeon-holed into a specific flowering season. With only a modicum of understandable overlap we have made out our flower lists and decided on our seasons in the same spirit.

To spring we have accorded three months, beginning half-way through February and finishing in mid-May. Summer takes over then and rolls over the country with sunshine, hollyhocks and roses in traditional style. Somewhere in the first days of September there is a change in the tempo, a sharper zest in the air that was not there before, so that we know that autumn has arrived and that we shall not see a real summer's day again until next year. For almost three months the countryside in this fresh season entertains us with its bright colours, until at about the end of November autumn stages a final blustery exit; the seasons change again for the last time in the year and winter has come. Although we are aware now of the nip in the early morning and accustom ourselves to the thought of winter, this is the most deceitful of all the seasons; sometimes very cold, sometimes quite mild. But whatever the weather, winter is a poor time for finding things to press, so we have taken you instead into the heated greenhouses and introduced you to ferns and 'foliage' plants which you will find to be new and most stimulating subjects for pressing.

We have illustrated our four flower seasons with pictures made in a wide variety of styles so as to suggest new starting points for your own work. This book is a natural progression from our first one on the subject. *Making Pressed Flower Pictures* took you through every step in the craft and encouraged you to follow detailed instructions and flower design patterns. In this second book, although we have given you one or two designs in each section which can easily be copied, most of our pictures are intended to spark off fresh ideas. We want to set the artist in you at work as well as to challenge your expertise with more advanced techniques.

There are four main seasonal chapters, each one dealing with pictures made only with the flowers of that season. There are comprehensive lists of flowers and leaves at the end of each section to help you in collecting materials for your press.

If you are a beginner in the world of flower pressing you will be able to find all the basic advice you need in the special information section in this book. It is arranged alphabetically and illustrated clearly with drawings, so that you can check on anything from flower presses to pressing grasses, or find out exactly how to fix pressed flowers on to card.

At the end of the book and of the year we have put together a cheerful collection of Christmas things, cards and calendars, tags and tablemats, and also a lovely picture made from flowers picked throughout the twelve months. After that you will not be able to resist getting out your boxes of pressed flowers and leaves and starting, with pleasure, on a new year of pressed flower pictures.

1 Spring

Spring is the first season of the year, but only a traveller from outer space could imagine that it starts in these northern islands on 1 January. Every new year is welcomed in with enthusiasm and, despite the cold weather, people soon begin to think of holidays and dream of warmer days. Gardeners indulge in dreams too, turning over yet again the pages of flower catalogues, ambitious for new ideas and tempted by the photographs of new varieties; but for the time being the countryside and gardens are brown and lifeless and all growth seems to have ceased. Cold winds and snow, rain and bitter frost strip and lay bare everything, and throughout January we are too busy keeping warm to think much about the spring. But every year when that unattractive month is past and the calendar assures us that February is half gone by, the days imperceptibly begin to change and reluctantly winter gives way to spring.

The birds seem to be aware of it first. The sparrows tumble about in the bare branches of the fruit trees, quarrelling in the pale sun, and the ducks flight down to their ponds in pairs, flying every morning with unswerving purpose across the still wintry sky and gliding down to search for food and nesting places in the half-frozen reeds.

Most mornings there is a hard white frost over the garden, the tall hellebores take daily punishment and at first glance it seems an inhospitable place for flowers. It looks as unprepossessing as it did at Christmas.. *Hamamelis molis, Prunus autumnalis* and the yellow aconites which cheered us in January are virtually over now, though the winter jasmine and pink and white winter heather are still in flower and there are some crocuses to add to the meagre amount of colour you can see from the sitting-room window.

This is the time of year when you must go out and search the garden for flowers. The hellebores, both *corsicus* and *foetidus,* and the snowdrops may stand up boldly in the open despite drooping every morning under with weight of frost, but the little spring flowers that are so beautiful enjoy being sheltered, and it can be like a treasure hunt to find them. Everything that is in flower now seems to be in hiding; the pink bergenia flowers lurk behind their wide leaves, the larger flowered hellebores, *H. atrorubens, H. niger* and *H. orientalis,* lean out cautiously from the shelter of the fence or friendly shrub, and as for the diminutive striped squill, pushkinia, the blue or white

Anemone blanda, even the single primrose and chionodoxa, you will practically have to get down on your hands and knees in order to find them, they grow so modestly.

Spring for the observer does indeed start just as soon as these little flowers begin to appear, and for the gardener too the month of February – at the end of a mild winter – provides work to be done. But for the reader of this book who wishes to start pressing flowers it is a time of impatience when material is hard to find. There is a scarcity of all flowers, and even of those that can be found only a few will press well, but above all one is reluctant to pick these small forerunners of the spring unless there is an abundance of them in the garden.

By the end of the month there will be very few full pages of blotting paper in your press. You will probably have a bright display of winter jasmine with some of the yellow florets pressed separately and others left on short stems with the unopened buds; you will have ivy leaves and grey tassels of *Garrya eliptica* side by side with a few of their oval leaves, and to fill another page you should be able to find enough snowdrops. These make a delicious display – fresh green and white – the flowers should be laid in profile with their leaves and upright buds beside them. All these flowers are from vigorous plants which can well spare some for your press. The heathers too, *Erica springwoodii*, will provide sufficient material to complete a page. They look spectacularly successful lying there on the white blotting paper, their colour and shape retained after they are dry – until you move them, and then half the little leaves drop off.

You will have to fill other pages in your press with assorted things, for there will probably not be enough of any one type of flower or leaf to fill a complete page on its own. Pick bright bergenia flowers and lay them in profile as well as full face, with a few heads of *Euphorbia wulfeni* and perhaps some precious blue flowers of grape hyacinth and *Vinca dubia*. The representatives of the hellebores will provide you with excellent pressing material; the flowers of *Helleborus niger*, *H. atrorubens*, *H. orientalis* as well as the smaller flowered *H. corsicus* and *H. foetidus* all press easily (the last one in the list has narrow purple banding on the edges of the petals and this is very effective). The panicle leaves of hellebores, which are so strangely shaped that they bring to mind some rare sea-creature, should be detached and pressed separately. You may have another page of more sombre colours drying out, a few *Iris stylosa* – which, if picked immediately they appear, may keep their dark purplish-blue – and the long racemes of *Mahonia japonica* which go into the press a pale yellow and emerge unexpectedly smoky-grey. Remember to pick some small heads of daphne and press the florets individually. Crocuses and little cyclamens will not figure much in your press, since their shapes do not lend themselves to being flattened.

At about this time of year you should be able to buy imported or 'forced' flowers from the shops. Buy yourself some mimosa, even though this French visitor is very expensive, and a bunch of the small

10

narcissus 'Soleil d'or', and lay them all carefully on the blotting paper. Concentrate on the flowers only; mimosa leaves rival only those of the heathers in their ability to shed bits and pieces, and the early narcissus are usually sold without theirs.

The most useful foliage at this time is the spiky leaves of the mahonia and the brown-blotched ivy leaves. Little else is out, and over-wintered leaves like those still hanging on the epimedium are invariably damaged. Only the roses will tentatively put out a fresh bronze leaf or two in these early chilly days – they are the supreme optimists in the garden.

Spring, however, is a most uncertain time of year. Suddenly there is a week of mild weather with sunny days when you can just feel a little warmth on your back as you walk in the garden, and in no time at all there are whole clusters of bright flowers on the primula plants. Now it can rain and blow and occasionally frighten you with a sharp frost, but daffodils and primula, doronicum and wallflowers have come out and their new colours replace those of the crocuses and snowdrops; the garden has more brightness in it now and, most important of all, there are many more flowers for you to add to your collection in the press. The shrubs are not to be outdone; japonica and forsythia, *Kerria japonica* and the glorious red of the flowering currant burst into bloom. Hyacinth and tulips, anemones and forget-me-not, followed by more and more daffodils, complete the effervescing colours of spring time.

At the end of this chapter on spring pressing there are lists of the garden and wild flowers which we have found most suitable (see pages 22–25). We give both the common and the Latin botanical names and occasionally suggest a variety which we think is particularly useful. There are also short notes for your guidance on any unusual preparation of flowers and foliage necessary before pressing. Shrubs and trees are included in our lists. We have illustrated our spring section with nine pictures made with flowers and foliage picked only during the months of late February, March, April and early May.

The wild-flower books announce authoritatively that the humble celandine – *Ranunculus ficaria* – flowers between March and May, so we have used it to make a very simple arrangement for you to copy. We have made it in the old fashioned 'botanical' style, and the drawing of the unframed design fixed on to a plain white background shows clearly the bright yellow stars and heart-shaped leaves of this wayside plant. The flowers are not difficult to press and in this case it is the simple approach that guides you – you press them straight from the plants, placing them in the press exactly as they were when they were growing. Some flowers will be open-faced and you will need to do nothing else but lay them straight down, while some will be half-opened and these must lie in profile, as will the buds and unformed seed heads. Remember the leaves, small and large, their reverse sides showing if necessary, and press enough to accompany your flowers.

Diagram 3 Completed design of
celandines

Diagram 4 Flowers and leaves
numbered in order of assembly

(Discard flowers which have been open for some time – they will dry white and lose their petals.)

We have drawn a breakdown of this spring picture for you to copy. There is a drawing of the complete arrangement first of all and then a collection of individually detailed flowers, numbered progressively in the order in which they were used in making the design (diagrams 3 and 4). At this point it is essential that you read carefully the instructions and advice given in the Information section on pages 92–96 under the main heading of 'Method of making flower pictures'. You will find two alternative ways described as 'Free' and 'Fixed', and it is purely a matter of personal preference which you follow. Once you have made your choice and fully understood the technique, you can prepare the base and background for this first little flower arrangement.

The instructions which follow, showing you how to make the celandine design, should also be used to guide you through the construction of the other pictures in this book for which we have drawn a breakdown and listed the flowers and leaves to be used.

1 Have ready the prepared base, your store of pressed material, tweezers, adhesive and frame.

2 Look carefully at the drawing of the completed design (diagram 3).

3 Identify the separate flowers in diagram 4 with their relevant position in diagram 3.

4 Using the itemised drawings to guide you, select and match up as closely as possible similar specimens from your own store. Place them ready on a piece of white paper.

5 Following the numbering system begin to make your design (following either the 'free' or 'fixed' method).

15cm
(6in)

There is another simple flower design for you to copy shown in diagram 5 which has a small 'bow' at its base. The soft colour of the pale green background mixes happily with the differing yellows of the flowers and must encourage anyone to copy it. It is perfect for springtime. The small bow around the stems has been cut from the petals of wallflowers. When making a 'bow', first draw one on thin white paper and cut it out, using small, sharp nail-scissors. Using this as a pattern, cut similar shapes from the pressed petals of a wallflower or tulip (See accompanying diagrams; the bow is about 3cm (1in) across.)

Our remaining pictures have been made not only to show the beauty of spring flowers but also to try to capture the flavour of this time of year. We have looked for inspiration in the delicacy of their colour and shape and in the fragility of leaf and bud.

The small picture in the maplewood frame (spring colour plate, top right) features the wild strawberry and, as with the celandine design, the same naturalistic idea has governed its making. You can observe, pick, press and finally re-create in a little picture like this a number of very common small plants. The coltsfoot, the daisy and the tiny ivy-leafed toadflax, to name but three, are suitable wild plants, while the snowdrop and *Anemone blanda*, both with a garden upbringing, will look equally charming treated in this way.

We have followed up and enlarged upon this simple idea of using the natural pattern of growth to give us inspiration. The long picture at the foot of the spring colour plate might be a patch of garden with early spring flowers growing sturdily upwards. There has been some artistic licence with the size of the *Helleborus atrorubens* and the others on the extreme right-hand side but basically the grape hyacinth, the anemones, the beautiful, pale rose-gold of the miniature tulips and the sparkling blue of the scillas and chionodoxas can be found like this in

Diagram 5 A spring posy containing primroses, anemones, mimosa and guelder rose, as well as ferns and clematis leaves, all tied with a 'bow' cut from wall-flower petals

13

any March garden. Around the feet of the cultivated flowers there are the earliest wild ones, tiny plants and ferns which seem to survive the rigours of late frosts quite easily. This long picture has a narrow silver-gilt frame and a pale cream mount; anything heavier would have overwhelmed the delicacy of the flowers.

Many of these early flowers grow from small bulbs and are happiest left quietly in the earth to flower from year to year. Some of them like the ordinary muscari, 'grape hyacinth', produces numerous seed-heads filled with black seeds and these, if left undisturbed, will scatter and start new colonies.

The idea of using a small oval frame is a particularly happy one when you have relatively few flowers to use. The oval-framed picture in the spring colour plate has a golden glow which throws into sharp relief the tracery of the black buds of elder. The blues of the forget-me-not and scillas blend contentedly with the many soft shades of primula and hellebores. There is a tip of mimosa at the bottom of the design and touches of *Viburnum opulus* and deutzia which widen the list of available flowers. We have made a drawing of this design and a breakdown of the flowers and their order of assembly to help you to make it (diagram 6).

In the middle of spring, when plants burst into flower as poets into verse, when cheerful yellow, blue and red fill the garden because the flowers outstrip the leaves in the race to meet the sun, it is in keeping to have a big picture full of lots of blooms. There are at least twenty-five different ones in the large gold-framed picture at the top left in the

Diagram 6 Contents:
 1. lily of the valley
 2. mimosa
 3. scilla
 4. hellebore bud
 5. primula bud
 6. primula
 7. laristinus buds
 8. berberis leaf
 9. ivy leaf
10. leaves of rue
11. primulas
12. daisy
Small extra trims where necessary

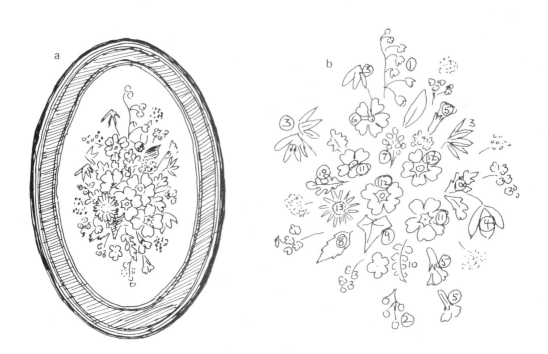

14

spring colour plate and they lie clustered together on a soft green background of satin (see also diagram 7). Early silver leaves of *Chrysanthemum haradjanii* and the dark ones of *Clematis montana* provide the two extremes in tone and the centre of the bouquet is held by a deep red cineraria and hellebores. Three of the popular hellebores are to be found in the pictures and they are very easy to press – *H. niger, H. orientalis* and *H. corsicus.* Notice the interesting outline ranging from the softness of ornithogalum and the miniature tulips to the bright buttons of mimosa and the profiles of dark primula. A design of this size must have good definition around the edge and against a background of colour this is especially important.

It is easy to overcrowd an arrangement, so when you are using a large number of flowers remember to leave sufficient open background around the design so that it can 'breathe'. The pressed flowers too must have contrasting shade and shape to avoid any suggestion of heaviness.

The visual benefits of contrasting shapes shows up in diagram 8 and figure 1. There are indeed a number of different flowers in this picture but the important thing is that they boast twenty or so different shapes of corolla between them. The eye can enjoy the difference between violaceae, rosaceae, umbellifereae, boraginaceae and scrophulariaceae, and can appreciate the graceful tilt of *Clematis montana* and compare it with the soft tails of *Garrya elliptica.* In the middle of the design there is a daisy-shaped doronicum next to a solid

Diagram 7 Flowers and leaves used in this picture include: mimosa, tulips, viola, hellebores, buttercups, wallflowers, daisy, heather, scilla, chionodoxa primula, forget-me-not, star of Bethlehem, cowslip, elder buds, auricula, cineraria exochorda, clematis, ivy and *Chrysanthemum haradjanii*

Diagram 8 A spring design illustrating many contrasting flower shapes

15

Figure 1 This picture has a rather ornate 'gold' frame and the flowers are fixed on to the cream background. There is plenty of colour here – a wide variety of flowers including strawberry. *Japonica mahonia* and Japanese cherry, Contents: broom – doronicum – anemone – clematis – cowslip – strawberry – japonica – pushkinia – deutzia – *Kerria japonica* – Japanese cherry – daisy – primula – *Ribes mahonia* – forget-me-not – hellebore – chionodoxa – scilla – columbine – *Garrya elliptica* – prunus – (foliage) ferns – euonymus – silverweed – *Clematis montana*

16

Figure 2 A modern gold frame with the flowers laid free on a cream silk base which has been padded with terylene. Contents: hellebores – primula – forget-me-not – lily-of-the-valley – grape hyacinth – snowdrop – tulip – mimosa – primrose – ornithogalum – elder – (foliage) euonymus – hellebore – rose – spiraea

Figure 3 A soft gold-flecked frame with the flowers mounted free on pale cream silk. It measures 28cm (11in) ×23cm (9in). Contents: hellebores – tulips – primulas – forget-me-nots – daisies – violas – (foliage) willow – tulip – alpine alchemilla – hellebore

little tulip and the pointed tips of aquilegia petals lie across a hellebore. Always consider the shapes of individual flowers when you are planning a picture.

Every spring it is disappointing not to be able to press daffodils successfully; we have found it well-nigh impossible to flatten one satisfactorily. The deep circular trumpet protrudes at right angles to the corolla frill and this means inevitably that from whichever angle it is pressed, one of the 'circles' will be crushed. The trumpet can be 'nicked' and persuaded to lie flat and the 'frill' can be folded behind the trumpet for a profile attempt, but you can never recapture fully the sturdy 'brass-band' appearance of this well-loved flower.

Every part of a plant, whether it is the flower and leaf on the stem or a cluster of buds, has a natural line of growth and if this has been retained in the pressing then it can be used as a starting point for the creation of a design. In figure 2 there is a perfect example of this. The picture is beautiful in its simplicity and yet there is a quite complicated network of graceful lines flowing through from one spray of flowers to another. To achieve this type of arrangement you will need to find two or three long-stemmed pieces of pressed flower or leaf material that still show their natural curve. They should be laid on the background so that this bend in their stems starts the flowing 'line' of an idea in your mind. Then you can add your flowers and leaves, buds and tendrils, relying on your artistic 'eye' to keep correct the continuation of the 'line' as well as the final balance of the whole design (diagram 9). In this picture, the starting points were the spiraea, the lily-of-the-valley, the mimosa and the small yellow primrose.

Our last 'fly-away' spring picture (figure 3) is very simple and would be lovely to copy. There is no attempt here to follow the way the flowers grow and no predefined ideas about style of design. It is a charming suggestion of spring, light and fresh and full of colour, and it is the flowers themselves that have inspired the arrangement (diagram 10).

Easter is the great festival in the Christian calendar and it is essentially associated with spring in this country. It needs little imagination to see that Easter time in many parts of the world has little to do with baby lambs and primroses – nor did it have anything to do with spring in Jerusalem in the year AD 32. Historically the date can only be fixed by the movements of the moon in relation to the Jewish passover. The dates of Easter day have been worked out far ahead and are listed in the prayer book. The earliest it can fall every year is 21 March and the latest is 25 April.

Diagram 9 Contents:
1. tip of spirea stem
2. mimosa
3. tulip
4. chionodoxa
5. tulip
6. lily of the valley
7. grape hyacinth
8. snowdrop
9. primula (dark crimson)
10. primula (yellow)
11. primula (apricot)
12. primula (crimson)
13. primula (yellow)
14. forget-me-not
15. hellebore foetidus
16. hellebore bud
17. hellebore leaves
18. hellebore orientalis
19. hellebore orientalis
20. elder buds

The old name of Easter was the Pascha of the Resurrection but one can understand the dilemma of the early churchmen in these islands who, faced with the unpalatable fact of an indigenous spring festival to the goddess 'Eastre' coinciding every year with the Pascha, had finally to allow a corruption of the pagan name to signal their new festival of the Resurrection. This is, of course, purely of academic interest to us, but it remains a fact that Easter, whether it falls late or early, must fall in springtime. Churches throughout the land will be full of flowers; vases of spring flowers and fresh green leaves will decorate the altars, fonts, window sills and chancel screens and fill the arched spaces with their scent. And there are small modest areas where arrangements of pressed flowers fixed on to Bible markers and pulpit falls can add their own decoration – beautiful miniatures of the swags of fresh flowers.

These minor hangings come under the general heading of Church Furnishings and are usually made of silk, often fringed and embroidered. At Easter the colour will be white or gold. Remember to choose pressed flowers which harmonise happily with the fresh ones to be used in decoration near by, and keep your design simple and bold in outline because most of the congregation will be sitting some way away. Always obtain permission from the priest or minister in charge of the church before planning anything.

You will find details of how to construct a bible marker or a fall as well as basic information about the traditional colours used in church furnishings in the Information section under the relevant alphabetical heading.

Diagram 10 A simple spring picture using hellebores, tulip, primula, forget-me-not, daisies and violas, with foliage from some of them

Garden flowers – Key to symbols

Plant type		Parts for pressing	
A	annual	b	buds
B	biennial	f	flowers
Bb	bulb	b&f	picked together
C	corms	l	leaves
Cl	climber	s	seed-head
F	fern	st.	stem
H	hardy	ten.	tendril
HH	half-hardy	f&l	picked together
P	perennial	*	plants that begin flowering in the spring and on into summer
Rp	rock plant		
Sh	shrub		
T	tree	**	those that continue to flower into autumn
Tb	tuber		
W	wild	(D)	difficult to press

Wild flowers – Key to symbols

Colour code

B	blue
Br	brown
Cr	cream
G	green
O	orange
P	pink
Pr	purple or mauve
R	red
W	white
Y	yellow
B&W	blue and white (bi-coloured)
B/W	flowers sometimes blue or white

Plants that can provide material for pressing all the year round

bramble	*Rubus fruticosus*	l
groundsel	*Seneccio vulgaris*	bf s
ivy	*Hedera helix*	ls
shepherd's purse	*Capsella bursa pastoris*	s

Common English Name	Botanical Name	Pressing Notes
alyssum (yellow) (P)	A. saxatile	f Useful strong colours
anemone (various) (Tb)	A. fulgens	fl Avoid old or very large flowers
	A. blanda	
	A. coronaria	
*aquilegia (various) (P)	A. vulgaris	f Cut away spurs and press flat
auricula (various) (P)	Primula auricula	f Rich colours very effective in designs
bergenia (pink) (P)		f Pick when first out
*broom (various) (Sh)	Cytisus	bf Choose buds and small flowers
brunnera (blue) (P)	B. macrophylla	f&b Press whole sprays
*ceanothus (blue) (Sh)	C. papillosus	b&f Clusters of buds give strongest blue
	C. rigidus	
chaenomeles (Japonica) (various) (Sh)	C. lagenaria	bf Needs hard pressing
chionodoxa (various) (Bb)		b Detach flowers and press separately
clematis (pink/white) (Cl)	C. montana	fl Leaves dry nearly black
*deutzia (pink) (Sh)		bf Whole sprays as well as single flowers
*doronicum (yellow) (P)	D. caucasicum	f Earliest yellow 'daisy' shape
*edelweiss (P)	Leontopodium alpinum	fl Grey velvety flowers and foliage
elder (cream) (T)	Sambucus nigra	bf Buds dry dark brown or black
epimedium (yellow) (P)	E. pinnatum	f Whole stems and single flowers
erica (various) (P)		b&f Small leaflets drop badly when dry
exochorda (white) (Sh)	E. giraldii	bf Press small sprays
flowering currant (pink/red) (Sh)	Ribes sanguineum	bfl Small flowering sprays only and small leaves
forget-me-not (blue/pink) (B)	Myosotis alpestris	b&f Sprays and single flowers
forsythia (yellow) (Sh)		f Single flowers – dry rather transparent
fritillaria (purple and cream) (Bb)	F. meleagris	f Bisect flowers and press separately
garrya (grey) (Sh)	G. elliptica	f Soft grey catkins
grape hyacinth (blue) (Bb)	Muscari armeniacum	b&fs Whole stems, avoid old flowers
guelder rose (cream) (Sh)	Viburnum opulus	f Use small clusters from large flowering heads
hellebore (various) (P)		bfl All varieties are excellent for pressing (remove pistil in old flowers and press separately)
ipheion (blue and white) (Bb)	I. uniflorum	f Transparent when dry use two together or mount

Kerria japonica (yellow) (Sh)		bf Use only very small flowers
*lily-of-the-valley (white) (P)	Convallaria majalis	bfl Press whole stems
mahonia (yellow) (Sh)	M. japonica	bfl Flowers dry blue grey
narcissus (various) (Bb)		bf Small and alpine varieties are best
ornithogalum (white) (Bb)	O. umbellatum O. nutans	f Dries a little transparent
osmanthus (white) (Sh)	O. delavayi	fl Use in clusters and singly
*periwinkle (blue) (P)	Vinca major V. minor	f Trim back of flower before pressing. Tends to fade
primula (various) (P)		bfl Red flowers dry dark brown
prunus (various) (T)		bf Use flowers freshly opened
pushkinia (white and blue) (Bb)	P. scilloides	f Press whole stems and single flowers
saxifrage (pink) (P) (London Pride)	S. umbrosa	f Use whole sprays
snowdrop (white) (Bb)	Galanthus nivalis	bfl Ensure flower heads press at correct angle
spurge (green and yellow) (P)	Euphorbia epithymoides	f Yellow bracts are unusual shape and colour
scilla (blue) (Bb)	S. siberica	f Good strong colour
strawberry (white) (P)		f Choose small side flowers
*tiarella (cream) (P)	T. cordifolia wherryi	fl Leaves are veined with dark red
tulip (various) (Bb)		fl Bisect small flowers only
viburnum (creamy white) (Sh)	V. carlesii (V. opulus see Guelder rose) V. tinus	f Press florets singly
*viola (various) (P)		f Flowers with strong colours only
wallflower (various) (B)		bf Small or half-opened flowers. Colours are good

WILD FLOWERS FOR PRESSING – SPRING

Common English Name	Botanical Name	Pressing Notes
*alkanet (B)	Pentaglottis sempervirens	f Small blue flowers are very delicate
*bird's-foot trefoil (Y&R)	Lotus corniculatus	f Useful strong colour
*black medick (Y)	Medicago lupulina	fl The flowers are very small indeed
*broom (Y)	Sarothamnus scoparius	bfl Press whole tips of stems – dries darker
*bugle (B)	Ajuga reptans	f Choose small complete heads
**bush vetch (P)	Vicia sepium	fl ten. Tendrils are excellent
buttercup (Y)	Ranunculus acris	bfl Newly opened flowers only
coltsfoot (Y)	Tussilago farfara	bf Flowers on stems

*common storksbill (P)	*Erodium circutarium*	bls The flowers are not worth pressing
*cow parsley (W)	*Anthriscus sylvestris*	fls Florets singly or in clusters
cowslip (Y)	*Primula veris*	fl Spread florets carefully or cut and press separately
**daisy (W&P)	*Bellis perennis*	bfl Include very small buds
**forget-me-not (B)	*Myosotis arvensis*	b&f Curly buds must lie in profile
*germander speedwell (B) (D)	*Veronica chamaedrys*	b Delicate petals – take extra care
*greater periwinkle (B)	*Vinca major*	fl Fairly rare in N. England; do not pick there
**herb Robert (P)	*Geranium robertinianum*	bfls Flowers are delicate. Late picked leaves colour
**horse-shoe vetch (Y)	*Hippocrepis comosa*	f Press flower head all in one
lesser celandine (Y)	*Ranunculus ficaria*	bfl Colour very bright. Old flowers dry white
*marguerite (W) (D)	*Chrysanthemum leucanthemum*	f Pick when first open. – a 'collar' may help with these
**pansy (Y Pr W)	*Viola tricolor*	bfl Cut stem off close to petals. Good colours
primrose (Y)	*Primula vulgaris*	bfl Trim away backs of large flowers before pressing
*ramsons (W)	*Allium ursinum*	bf delicate petals once they are dry
**red campion (R)	*Silene dioica*	f Colour often fades – press more than you do usually
snowdrop (W)	*Galanthus nivalis*	pfl Preserve the natural 'droop' of the flowers in profile
*star of Bethlehem (W) (D)	*Ornithogalum umbellatum*	f Press florets separately, dries semi-transparent
*stitchwort (W) (D)	*Stellaria holostea*	bfl Very delicate
*violet (Pr)	*Viola odorata* *Viola riviniana*	bfl Cut stem away and press separately. Profile and full face
*water avens (P&Br)	*Geum rivale*	bf Ensure flower heads tip downwards on stem
*wild strawberry (W)	*Fragaria vesca*	fls Half-formed fruits press well
wood anemone (W)	*Anemone nemorosa*	fl Cut flowers and leaves off main stem, press and reassemble
wood spurge (G)	*Euphorbia amygdaloides*	f Press small pieces for unusual colour

LEAVES FOR PRESSING – SPRING

artemisia
ceonothus
Clematis montana
euonymus
ferns
ivy
jasmine

lupin
mahonia
myrtle
rose
sage
spiraea
Chrysanthemum haradjanii

2 Summer

a

b

Comparing the flowers and their seasons to the tides of the sea, summer must be full high tide. The first surging growth of spring has changed in character and between the months of May and June nature reaches a new maturity. There is far more foliage on everything and throughout most gardens plants stand high, shoulder to shoulder; there is a fresh pattern of colour abroad, more trees and shrubs blossom and in the borders and the rockeries there are many new flowers. Without doubt there has been a change of season and without a fanfare summer has arrived. There are long days – hot and sunny in a good year – and by early August every plant seems to have reached its allotted size and desires only to finish flowering and to fruit and ripen in the sun.

Although there are some plants which will continue to flower through spring and summer, generally speaking you will find that there is a great change in the style of the newcomers. A shade more vulgar perhaps in their colours, trying to eclipse each other with brighter and yet brighter shades. The emphasis seems to be on pink, red, purple and orange now, in stripes and blotches, bi-colour and even tri-colour, and what nature does not achieve by herself the plant breeder does instead. There is, too, a greater flamboyance in the size and shape of the blooms; they vie with each other in the crowded beds for space and attention: irises and roses, paeonies and double poppies, voluptuous lilies and lupins of every conceivable shade. Sadly these big summer beauties do not figure in our list of garden flowers to press, they are nearly all too large and thick and instead of drying satisfactorily will only attract mould. Many of the favourite annuals too, such as sweet William, stocks and scarlet salvias should be picked to fill your vases only. If you should find a very small lily and can bisect

c

Diagram 11
a. allium
b. lily
c. viola
d. love-in-a-mist
e. phlox
f. lady's mantle

26

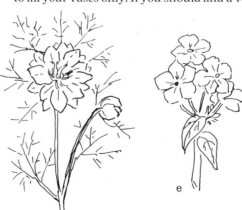

d

e

f

Figure 4 An oval modern frame 41cm (16in) high and a design of
grasses, leaves, ferns, seed-heads and buds mounted by the 'fixed' method
on a cotton background. They have been arranged in a simple 'bunch'
and the stalks have been assembled and stuck down last of all. Contents:
(seeds) candytuft – cow-parsley – hog-weed – (buds) spiraea – boccania –
scabious – nettles – sorrel – plantain – senecio (leaves) – wild raspberry –
rush – thistle – acer – ferns – grasses – bramble – anthemis – willow –
lupin – hawthorn

it or like to experiment with a few sprays of lilac or the top dark buds of weigelia then do so, for it is important to try out new material in your press.

In the summer you must, comparatively speaking, think small and press small. Look round the shady side of the plants for the little flower heads and wait until the big first shoots with the large flowers are over, cut them back and then pick the smaller second ones which come on the side shoots. Of course there are a great number of garden plants with modest sized flowers which can be picked and pressed successfully – a glance at our flower lists at the end of the section suggests them.

Country wild flowers too in the hot months have a habit of growing in great profusion. In the fields you will find masses of scarlet poppies and chamomile, and when the heather and the meadow-sweet are out whole hillsides are spread with purple and the damp places in the valleys smothered with cream. This, then, is an easy time for picking wild flowers for your press, there is such an abundance of common varieties. Nevertheless it will repay you to study our second list on pages 36–40 carefully rather than pick and press everything that pleases your eye.

Our first choice of summer pictures is the one of poppies and grass featured in the summer colour plate (top right) because it succeeds in catching instantly the feeling of summer walks and picnics in the fields. The grass and leaves will have been simple to press (diagram 14) but the flowers have had to be backed to counter their transparency. Once this has been done the arrangement is not a difficult one to repeat, since the natural tilt of the poppy-heads – if they have been pressed carefully – will direct the placing of both flowers and grasses and the accompanying leaves.

This style of flower picture lends itself well to repetition, and a series of four or even six using the same frame, mount and base with different flowers would be very attractive hung together on a wall. The picture of small roses (diagram 15) which is also shown in the summer colour plate – despite the different coloured background – bears this out and the two make charming companions.

Diagram 12
a. poppy
b. mugwort

Diagram 13
a. verbena
b. agapanthus
c. salpiglossis
d. lily-of-the-valley

Summer annuals can, if their size is moderate, provide an excellent colour range for pressing. Lobelia and nemophila, despite the fact that blue is often a fugitive shade, hold theirs well in the press, mauve is covered by ageratum and small pansies, while verbena and candytuft can provide bright spots of different colours. Even the common-or-garden single marigolds and tagetes can be picked and used. Our list will suggest others.

There is one group of well-loved flowers which are not always good candidates for your press: these are the roses. Our very pretty picture in the summer colour plate (top left), made solely with the two small roses 'Canary bird' and 'American pillar', would seem to belie this, but in fact many more roses are unsuitable for pressing than are not, their unsuitability being entirely due to their size and thickness. The average H.T. garden rose will never succumb to being flattened. Most single roses, however, press well and their buds can be bisected successfully. Very small double roses – the miniature varieties are best – should have some of the centre petals removed before pressing so that the attractive stamens show. Small and single are the two factors you should follow where roses are being considered. Wild ones that grow in the hedges, such as the beautiful sweet briar or eglantine, to give its other name, are ideal because they comply in both features.

Leaves and grasses can be viewed only too easily as mere appendages to the bright petals, but we have made a large picture (figure 4) to encourage you to pick, press and use such material for its own sake. There are fourteen different sorts of foliage ranging from the prickly leaf of the thistle to the silvery underside of a wild raspberry leaf. Dried seed-heads of candytuft and hogweed provide unusual shapes, and the only true 'flowers' in this picture are the dark tassels of

Diagram 14 Poppies

Diagram 15 Roses

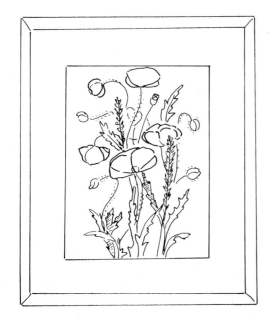

29

stinging-nettle and some red-brown flowering spikes of sorrel. This foliage arrangement has been mounted on a coarse, inexpensive cotton background using the 'fixed' method.

The range of shade and tone in a picture such as this last one will be much narrower than in one made from summer flowers. The oval design in diagram 16 and the summer colour plate show a wonderful variety of mixed blossoms held together with their stalks in a little basket; every colour in the spectrum seems to be here. The idea of using colour itself as the point of inspiration for your designs must always be considered. You can combine many shades together, as in this picture, or it can be the contrast between two or more shades that pleases your eye, or lastly it may be the fact that one shade compliments or 'goes' with another. Flower designs can be created using any one of these ideas, and we have made one in blues and greys, also in the colour plate, to illustrate the last (diagram 17). The background is a neutral ivory which does not detract from overall soft shades.

Remember the vegetables when you hunt in your garden for things to press. Leaves from the humble carrot and sage, for example, will fit happily into any design, and when your onions rush away to seed let them bloom in peace and try pressing some of the tiny florets.

Another garden flower design for you to make is featured in diagram 18. The flowers and leaves are set inside a mount and again we have listed them in the order in which they were used to make the design.

We have made a picture almost entirely of wild flowers picked with foliage and grasses and ferns in August. The black and white photograph (figure 5) shows the interesting 'spiky' silhouette and we

Diagram 16
a. Mixed summer flowers
b. Small fronds of bracken, well pressed, have been used to make this flower container

have also given you a drawing and a 'breakdown' of the individual items and their names (diagram 19) so that you can easily copy it. None of the flowers are rare or even difficult to find and you should be able to return home from most summer holidays in Britain with these flowers in your press. Should you have difficulty in finding any particular item, pick something else of a similar size and colour; for example, the white daisy-type flowers in the centre with the rather greyish centres are in fact sneezewort, *Achillea ptarmica*; but if you cannot find this plant then substitute another, such as one of the chamomiles or the feverfew. They will be just as good.

Holiday pictures are always fun to make and can remind you for years of the sunny days you enjoyed. (You will, incidentally, never be able to remind yourself of that disastrous wet week you endured in the so-called summer of '81 – flowers picked in the rainy weather grow mouldy in the press – so that even your masochism will be thwarted!) If you are travelling overseas remember that many countries nowadays are endeavouring to bring in laws to spare rare plants from possible extinction. The list of protected plants in the U.K. now contains 61 varieties, many of them already so rare that you are unlikely to come across them (see *protected varieties* in the Information

Figure 5 Summer wild flowers picked in the west country. The colours are muted except for a single small buttercup. There is purple in the heather and cream in the meadowsweet and the reverse of the fern shows the dark brown of ripe spores. The outline of this picture is very definite and pleasing to the eye

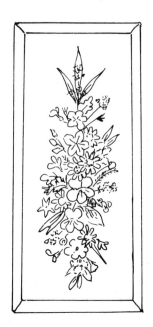

section, p. 19). We suggest that before you embark on any serious picking of countryside flowers you learn how to recognise them with the help of a good botanical book. It is an offence to pick any part of these listed plants.

Whenever you pick wild flowers for pressing, never just touch one solitary flower or take much foliage from a single plant. Even when there are a number of similar plants growing together you should keep uppermost in your mind the understanding that plants need their leaves to live and that their flowers are essential for reproduction. One less flower-head means less seeds for the following year.

Think before you pick.

Ask yourself – can the plant spare it?

We have two more pictures in our summer collection. Diagram 20, which is very different from the others, shows how you can use a modern style 'Klipframe' to hold the pressed flowers. The poppies and grasses featured here seem to have an extra dimension to them which is brought about by the depth of the perspex. There are nine different grasses here, and combined with the poppies they show how very charming such material can look, even though the flowers them-

32

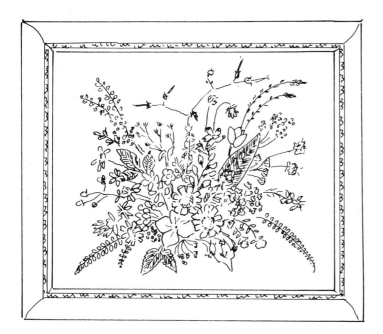

Diagram 19 Contents:
1. herb Robert
2. ferns
3. chenopodium
4. vervain
5. nettles
6. traveller's joy
7. St John's wort
8. meadow sweet
9. heather and ling
10. bugle
11. reverse side of fern
12. yarrow
13. valerian
14. rush
15. Japanese anemone
16. hogweed
17. hydrangea
18. sneezewort
19. montbretia
20. wild thyme
21. borage
Trims: senecio buds – thrift –
scilla autumnalis – buttercup – fennel
– groundsel

selves are very ordinary. They have been stuck on the base loose using the 'fixed' method and are held in place by the spring clips which hold the two surfaces together.

The last picture, figure 6 (the arrangement also features on the front jacket), gives us a feeling of the sweet abundance of summer flowering plants that pleases us every year. The warm brown of the wood of the antique oriental frame is a perfect surround for the bright colours, while the pale cream of the background allows the curly tendrils and tight buds and leaves to make an interesting outline. There are old-fashioned flowers like lavender, marguerites and roses, more exotic blooms such as the Passion flower and humble ones like herb Robert and ferns from the countryside.

It is hardly surprising that the poet wrote so blithely about 'sumer icumen in' – nobody can look forward to its departure and the loss of all the flowers.

Figure 6 More than twenty different summer flowers are clustered together to remind you of the abundance of this season. They are fixed down on to fine cream terylene, the whole surrounded by an antique oriental frame. It is quite large and measures 44cm (17in) by 34cm (13½in). Contents: roses – lavender – herb Robert – potentilla – astrantia – spiraea – marguerite – ixia – ceanothus – polygonum – cornflower – love-in-a-mist – Japanese anemone – passion flower – nemophila – verbena – daisy – thyme – honeysuckle – bocconia – delphinium – cow-parsley – *Carpentaria californica* – a wide variety of leaves. (This picture is also featured, without its frame, on the front jacket.)

Diagram 20 Poppies and grasses in a modern frame

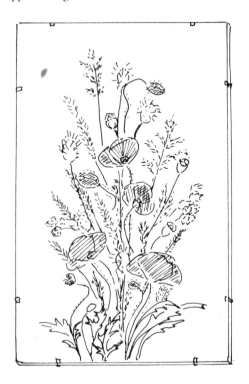

Common English Name	Botanical Name	Pressing Notes
Agapanthus (blue/white) (P)		f Press florets singly and in profile (blue only)
ageratum (blue) (HHA)		f Clusters
alchemilla (green) (P)	*A. mollis*	f Sprays of minute green flowers
	A. alpina	l Press leaves for silver reverse side
allium (various) (Bb)		f Whole heads of small varieties, otherwise single flowers
alyssum (various) (A)		f Whole stems to be pressed
**anaphalis (white) (P)		bf Single flowers and clusters
anchusa (blue/purple) (P)	*A. azurea*	bf Press single flowers and curving
(A)	*A. capensis*	buds
**anemone (pink/white) (P)	*A. japonica*	bf Old and large flowers tend to fade
anthemis (white) (P)	*A. cupiana*	fl Flowers and leaves excellent
(yellow)	*A. tinctoria*	
astrantia (green/white) (P) (Hattie's pincushion)	*A. maxima*	f All sizes press very well
**caryopteris (blue) (Sh)		f Small flower sprays
**catmint (blue) (P)	*Nepeta × faassenii*	bfl Lavender blue spikes very useful
ceanothus (blue) (Sh)	*C. azureus*	f Fluffy blue clusters
**ceratostigma (blue) (Sh)	*C. willmottianum*	f Vivid blue. Seldom fades
chrysanthemum (various) (A)	*C. carinatum*	f Choose small flowers only
clary (pink/blue) (A)	*Salvia horminum*	l Coloured leaves or bracts dry excellently
clematis (various) (P)		fls Small flowers and buds and seedheads later
delphinium (various) (P)		bf Individual flowers or sprays (white is disappointing)
dicentra (red) (P) (bleeding heart)		f Sprays
exochorda (white) (Sh) (pearl bush)	*E. giraldii*	fb Masses of white flowers – unusual
**fuchsia (various) (Sh)		bf Bisect flowers. The long stamens and pistil very delicate
gentian (blue) (P)		f Colour usually preserved after drying
geranium (various) (P)		f Tends to fade
godetia (various) (A)	*G. grandiflora*	f Tends to dry transparent. Very fragile
gypsophila (various) (A)	*G. elegans*	bf Sprays – very graceful
(P)	*G. panticulata*	
heliotrope (blue) (P) (cherry pie)	*H. peruvianum*	bf Clusters
**heuchera (pink/red) (P)	*H. sanguinea*	bf Sprays

**honeysuckle (various) (Sh)	*Lonicera*	f Flowers turn brown in press
**hydrangea (various) (Sh)		f Flowers single and clusters
**hypericum (yellow) (Sh) (St. John's wort)		f Remove seed box and pistil if necessary from flower centre
**jasmine (white) (Sh)	*J. officinale*	bfl Every part presses well. Leaves turn darker
larkspur (various) (A)	*Delphinium ajacis*	bf Single flowers or sprays
lavender (blue) (Sh)	*Lavendula spica*	bfl Press whole spikes
lily (various) (Bb)		f Use only small flowers – bisect if necessary
limnanthes (various) (A)	*L. douglasii*	Petals become transparent. Mount on tissue
linum (blue) (P)	*L. usitatissimum*	bst. Flowers very fragile. Press curving stem and buds
**lobelia (blue) (HHA)	*L. erinus*	bf Vivid blue is retained
(red) (P)	*L. fulgens*	fl Flowers dry dark. Leaves purple
loosestrife (yellow) (P)	*L. punctata*	f Star-shaped flowers
love-in-a-mist (blue/white) (A)	*Nigella damascena*	f Remove seed box before pressing
love-lies-bleeding (red and green) (A)	*Amaranthus caudatus*	f Tends to fade
marigold (yellow/orange) (A)	*Calendula officinalis*	f Petals fragile when dry – extra care needed
myrtle (cream) (Sh)	*M. communis*	fl Shiny leaves are useful
nemophila (blue) (A) (baby blue eyes)	*N. insignis*	f Clear blue – dries transparent sometimes
**passion flower (white/green/blue) (Cl)	*Passiflora cerulea*	fl Cut out pistil and stigma and press separately
perovskia (blue) (Sh)	*P. atriplicifolia*	f Delicate flower spikes
phacelia (blue) (A)	*P. campanularia*	f Very effective colour
phlox (various) (HHA)	*P. drummondii*	f Trim flower at the back if necessary
	P. panticulata	f Useful star-shaped flowers
potentilla (P) (red)	*P. atrosanguinea*	f scarlet turns to crimson when dry
(various) (Sh)	*P. fruticosa*	f Very easy to press
primula (various) (P)		bf Press flowers singly
rose (various) (Sh) 'canary bird' (yellow) 'wedding day' (white) 'American pillar' (pink) 'Rosa rubifolia' (pink/purple) All miniature varieties		bfl Buds when thick should be bisected. Double roses should have centre petals removed to show stamens
rudbeckia (pink) (P)	*Echinacea purpurea*	f Useful daisy – press very hard
sage (blue/mauve) (P)	*Salvia officinalis*	fl Flowers are difficult. Leaves are excellent
spiraea (pink) (Sh)	*S. x bumalda*	bfl Buds turn almost black. Flowers

'Anthony Waterer'

WILD FLOWERS FOR PRESSING – SUMMER section and preceding table:

Common English Name	Botanical Name	Pressing Notes
spurge (various) (P)	Euphorbia	l Small coloured leaves or bracts
tellima (green to pink) (P)	T. grandiflora	fl Press whole spikes
tobacco plant (various) (HHA)	Nicotiana offinis	f Pick small flowers. Press flat but trim back
veratrum (purple/black) (P)	V. nigrum	f Very dark stars – dries black
verbascum (various) (P)	V. hybridium	f Press single flowers
verbena (various) (HHA)	V. hybrida	f Whole heads or single flowers are easy to press
xeranthemum (white or mauve) (A)		f Everlasting flowers
yarrow (various) (P)	Achillea filipendulina A. ptarmica	f Break flower heads into small pieces

(top right continuation: "dry brown. Young leaves are cream and pink")

WILD FLOWERS FOR PRESSING – SUMMER

Common English Name	Botanical Name	Pressing Notes
agrimony (Y)	Agrimonia eupatoria	fl Yellow spikes – press complete
alkanet (B)	Pentaglottis sempervirens	f Delicate flowers
**bird's-foot trefoil (Y)	Lotus corniculatus	bfl Very useful colours
**black medick (Y)	Medicago lupulina	fs Miniature yellow clovers
comfrey (various)	Symphytum officinale	f Keep buds in curling shapes
corn chamomile (W)	Anthemis arvensis	bfl Discard old flowers
**cow wheat (Y)	Melampyrum pratense	f&l Dries black
creeping cinquefoil (Y)	Potentilla reptans	fl Leaves are silver grey
**fat hen (Gr)	Chenopodium album	f Flowers in grey spikes
**fennel (Y)	Foeniculum vulgare	fl Yellow florets press well
**feverfew (W)	Chrysanthemum parthenium	fl Flowers retain whiteness
**field scabious (B)	Knautia arvensis	f Old flowers will fade
flowering rush (P)	Butomus umbellatus	f Press pink florets singly
greater celandine (Y)	Chelidonium majus	f Remove seeds and pistil if necessary
guelder rose (Cr)	Viburnum opulus	fb Press flowers singly and in clusters
**honeysuckle (Cr)	Lonicera periclymenum	fb Pick young flowers
ivy-leafed toadflex (W/B)	Cymbalaria muralis	bfls Ends of trailing stems to be pressed whole
lady's mantle (G)	Alchemilla vulgaris	fl Useful, unusual colour

**mallow (Pr)	*Malva sylvestris*	f Delicate and difficult
meadow cranesbill (R) (Pr)	*Geranium pratense*	fl Flowers uncertain Leaves good
meadowsweet (Cr)	*Filipendula ulmaria*	b&f Best picked when just out. Buds very useful
melilot (Y)	*Melilotus officinalis*	b&f Useful yellow spikes
milkwort (B)	*Polygala vulgaris*	f Blue usually retained
**nipplewort (Y)	*Lapsana communis*	bf Round buds dry black
Ox-eye daisy (W) (marguerite)	*Chrysanthemum leucanthemum*	f Press very hard ('collar' may help)
pennywort (G)	*Umbilicus rupestris*	b&f Unusual green spikes
poppy (R)	*Papaver rhoeas*	bf Dries rather transparent, will need a double or a mount
raspberry (W)	*Rubus idaeus*	l Silver underside to leaves, flowers very difficult
rock rose (Y)	*Helianthemum chamaecistus*	bfl Very fragile – take extra care
rose (dog) (P/W)	*Rosa canina*	bfl Pick young flowers. Bisect buds
**rosebay willowherb (Pp)	*Epilobium agustifolium*	bf Single flowers and spike of buds
sheep's bit scabious (B)	*Jasione montana*	f Old flowers fade
sheep's sorrel (Br&R)	*Rumex acetosella*	b&f Needs gentle handling
silverweed (y)	*Potentilla anserina*	l Beautiful silver-grey leaves
**slender St John's wort (Y)	*Hypericum pulchrum*	f Press flower spikes
small scabious (B)	*Scabiosa columbaria*	f Half opened flowers are good
sneezewort (W)	*Achillea ptarmica*	bf Excellent flowers to press
stinging nettle (G)	*Urtica dioica*	fl Flower tassels dry black
sundew (W)	*Drosera rotundifolia*	f Useful spiky flowers
sweet briar (P)	*Rosa rubiginosa*	bfl Young flowers, bisect buds
**tansy (Y)	*Tanacetum vulgare*	bf Press hard
thrift (P)	*Armeria maritima*	fl Easy to press
thyme (P)	*Thymus drucei*	f&l Pick whole stems
traveller's joy (G)	*Clematis vitalba*	bfl Very easy to dry
umbelliferae (most varieties) (W/P)		bfs Press whole heads and single florets

vetch (bitter) (R&Pp)	*Lathyrus montanus*	f Ensure flowers are in profile ften. (as above)
vetch (common) (P&B)	*Vicia sativa*	
vetch (tufted) (P&B)	*Vicia cracca*	b&fl Stretch out tendrils once to untangle
**water mint (P)	*Mentha aquatica*	b Choose flowers with young leaves
**white bryony (G)	*Bryonia dioica*	flten. Press flowers carefully
wild chamomile (W)	*Matricaria recutita*	bf Needs hand pressing
**wild pansy (Y&R)	*Viola tricolor*	bfl Very easy. Trim stem
wild strawberry (W)	*Fragaria vesca*	fls Half formed fruit very attractive
woody nightshade (Y/Pp)	*Solanum dulcamara*	f Stems of buds and flowers
**yarrow (W, occ.P)	*Achillea millefolium*	fl Pink or white. Very useful

LEAVES FOR PRESSING – SUMMER

Green
anemone
bracken
carrot
caryopteris
dianthus
ferns
hedge maple

hellebores
herb Robert
lavender
lily-of-the-valley
passion flower
pulsatilla
rose

sycamore
traveller's joy
white bryony
wild strawberry
Virginia creeper
yarrow

Dark Green
broom
clematis montana
ivy

jasmine
mugwort
myrtle

nettle
traveller's joy
violets

Red or Brown
acer (Japanese maple)
copper beech

cotinus
epimedium

pieris

Grey
Alchemilla alpina
Anthemis cupiana
artemisia
Potentilla anserina

pyrethrum
rue
sage
Santolina chamaecyparissus

Senecio greyii
Stachys lanata
Senecio maritima
tanacetum
willow

Variegated
euonymus   elaeagnus   spiraea   tiarella

3 Autumn

Autumn is the time of year, if artists and poets are to be believed, when colour is all, when scarlet and vermilion, gold and rich brown mixed together on a giant's palette transform the trees. In a year when summer lingers on and the older generation declare an 'Indian Summer', when the days are still hot and dry and it is sharp and cool only at night, then the leaves of tree, shrub and creeper turn slowly to their autumn shades and can achieve a spectacular display.

The gardener will be aware that there is little substance in this majestic colouring for him, he knows that time is against him and that once the harvest is over these bright leaves will soon be blown away and there will be nothing left for him to do but begin the slow process of tidying the garden and preparing for the winter. This time of year however is an exciting time for the reader of this book who is really interested in experimenting with new effects of colour and size in pressed flower design.

Flowers are admittedly at a premium in these late months. There are the old stalwarts left from the summer annuals which are putting out a second or even a third batch of flowers – marigolds and lobelia for example will good-naturedly continue to bloom – but overall the number of reliable flower heads suitable for pressing will have greatly diminished. The true latecomers, such as fuchsias and hydrangeas, are excellent to press, and although the majority of chrysanthemums and Michaelmas daisies are too large to press and use in all but a few pictures, you may be able to include some of the smaller heads. Instead it is to the bright, flamboyant leaves that you should turn your attention at this time of year, and the flowers must surely take second place to them. Then your imagination will find inspiration in the fanning out of the scarlet foliage of the sumach, *Rhus typhina,* or else in combining red, green and gold in a vain attempt to emulate the glory of a Virginia creeper. The woods and the hedgerows as well as the gardens will be ablaze with colour to give you fresh ideas.

The actual techinque of pressing these highly coloured leaves is the same as for flowers and it is just as essential to pick them at the correct moment. Watch the deepening colour in the leaves of creepers and trees carefully; ideally you pick the leaf as soon as it has reached its full colour and before it has separated from the wood. Leaves that are left too long on the trees or are picked up from the ground usually emerge from the press crinkled and rough-surfaced and are seldom worth the

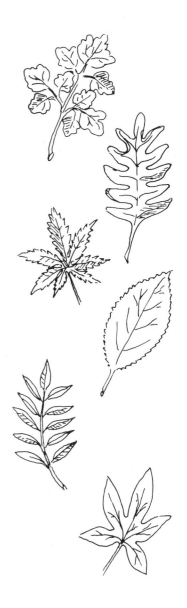

Diagram 21 Leaves

41

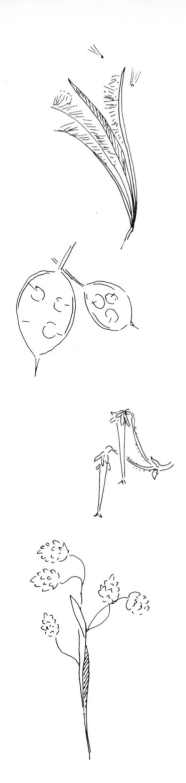

trouble of collecting. Always inspect your leaves critically – a damaged outline or a bruised surface will show up even more distinctly when it is pressed paper-thin. Pick on a dry day and get them into the press as soon as you can.

There is another area of autumn pressing which is very much worthwhile and that is in the ripe seed-heads of some plants. The members of the clematis family nearly all produce whirls of feathery seeds which are rewarding to press. The small, hardly-formed berries of many shrubs are surprisingly effective in pictures; they should be picked in early autumn before they become too juicy. The opening seeds of willow-herb can give a most unusual shape, although it is very hard to catch one before the two halves spring back too far. The small dark pods of vetch, the pointed capsules of herb Robert and the seed-heads of the late flowering umbelliferae such as fool's parsley and fennel are all worth picking and gently pressing. The round pods of honesty, *Lunaria annua*, will be ripe and ready for picking by this time. Pick the pods complete with the stalks and hang them in bunches upside-down to dry. When they are completely crisp to touch, take them down and rub the circular seed-pods one at a time between your fingers. This will detach the two outside covers and release the seeds, exposing the silvery centre panel. (Keep the seeds to plant in your garden for next year.) You can use these shining circles in your flower designs to great effect. All these different shaped seed-heads will give you a fine variety of ornamental shapes to use.

Put as many different shades of autumn leaves into the press as you can find and remember too to select ones of unusual size and shape. Pick the silver-grey ones which will still be growing in your garden such as senecio, the rock *Alchemilla alpina* and the creeping cinquefoil, and do not overlook the ferns, which should continue to grow until the cold weather arrives in earnest. Bracken, when it has turned golden and brown in October, will also begin to curl up at the ends of the fronds – these can look charming in a picture.

Collect and put aside hydrangea florets and agapanthus pods and any other material that you are going to 'skeletonise'. The 'bone-white' tracery of the leaf veins can make delicate additions to autumn and winter pictures.

In the pictures which we have made for our autumn section we have attempted to show you how to form designs using a wide selection of the different plant material which is available from the end of September through October to the last dead days of November. The trees and shrubs in your garden will come into their own and offer you colourful leaves to press. Some of these leaves are so intensely bright in shade that they would of necessity clash with each other if they were to be placed all together in a design, but you will find that if you are selective in your choice and use leaves and flowers of similar or of complementary shades, then you can still achieve lovely autumnal effects and avoid garishness. The long picture in the autumn colour plate and in diagram 23 is a good example of this; the various strong

Diagram 22 Seedheads

Figure 7 The old, gold-leaf frame is probably Victorian and measures 34cm (13½in) by 30cm (12in). Although the pink gesso shows through in places it has not been touched up. The distinctive shapes of the various yellow leaves show up very well against the black. The strong stalks of the ivy and clematis seed-heads have had to be stuck down firmly. The crisp leaves still remind one of the fallen leaves in the woods. Contents: *Robinia pseudoacacia* – pampas – ginkgo – clematis – ivy – sycamore – azalea – bracken – honesty – santolina – beech – fennel

Figure 8 The pale gold of the background shows up well the soft colours of the leaves. Strong colour lies in the darkened hydrangea flowers and in the drift of red berberis leaves. Canary bird flowers repeat the gold shade at the focal point. The frame is plain silver, 45cm (18in) by 30cm (12in) and the pressed material was fixed with adhesive

1. Four pictures made with spring flowers. Two of the frames are modern and
two are antique. The largest one is 38cm (15in) x 31cm (12¼in) and the flowers
have been arranged on a green silk base using the 'free' method. In the bottom
picture the flowers have been fixed on to the white background with an adhesive

2. The four summer pictures epitomise the hottest months of the year. Roses and poppies fill the two identical gold frames and the green mounts set off the green leaves. The oval picture is a summer mélange and the basket is made from bracken fronds. A quite different note is struck by the soft greys and blues of the remaining picture

shades of red in the fuchsias, hydrangeas, Virginia creeper and sumach leaves combine well in tone and are set off by the pale silk background, while the cerulean blue flowers of that attractive small shrub the ceratostigma highlight the strong, dominant reds. Introducing another autumn shade such as yellow or brown into this particular picture would spoil it. Save the leaves of those shades for another time.

The picture in figure 7 is a further example of careful colour selection. This time the shades of the leaves and seedheads are in fact yellow, brown, cream or black. The gold, coin-like leaves of the *pseudoacacia* are unusual, and so are the darker yellow triangles from the ginkgo tree, but laid on a neutral black background they will combine happily with almost any shade of brown. Autumn leaves in this familiar tint are to be found in abundance, and it is a simple matter therefore to add sycamore, bracken, azalea and beech to complete the design. Add clematis seed-heads, ivy and a cream tuft of pampas and there is a colour range here which is pleasing to the eye.

In our spring and summer designs we have seen that very strong colour is often used most successfully when it is introduced sparingly; two vivid, scarlet roses near the centre of a design or a single orange marigold at the focal point, for example, will be sufficient to enliven a picture. The same pattern of colour contrast holds good for autumn foliage. Figure 8 is an example of this; the dark red acer leaves and bright hydrangea florets are placed in the solid centre of the design, but this centre is surrounded by the grey-green leaves of the *Lawsonia columnaris* and the soft yellow of a late-flowering *Potentilla fruticosa*. The red is muted and the overall effect much softer. Silver-grey leaves like senecio can also be used like this in conjunction with bright red shades.

Search out the small leaves and press them too; there will be a fine variety of miniature autumn-shaded foliage and, as can be seen from the two rectangular pictures in our autumn colour plate, these

Diagram 23 A panel picture of strong autumn colours

Diagram 24 Leaves of: clematis – blackberry – rose – pieris – cranesbill – honesty – pinks – fern – willow – rock alchemilla – creeping buttercup – maple – mahonia – bracken – spirea; with honesty, grasses and bursting seedheads of willowherb

45

Diagram 25 Pressed material includes flowers of poppies which have been backed with dark red tissue paper, fuchsia and hydrangea, mixing the red and green. The dark green leaves of jasmine give movement to the design while the sumach and berberis leaves provide real autumnal crimson. The tiny heads of *Skimmia japonica* flowers are unusual for this time of year

smaller-sized designs, featuring mainly leaves, can be as charming and redolent of this time of year as the larger ones (diagram 24). Once more one sees that flowers are not always essential and that a mixture of small, unspectacular leaves artistically arranged on a background of pale cream or of yellow silk can capture the feeling of the autumn months. Grey foliage is used very successfully in both of these designs. Soft colours make the best backgrounds for these smaller designs; when you are using larger leaves and flowers such as the red poppies in the oval picture (diagram 25), a dark background can be used to great effect. Here it is green satin, which combines with the bright leaves to make a strong mixture of red and green.

We have already mentioned seeds and berries which can be pressed successfully. Figure 9 and diagram 26 illustrate this well. Notice the V-shaped seed-capsules of the willowherb as well as a ripened head of clematis. Berries, small and black, are included here too and are very effective. Unfortunately few berries take kindly to a press once they are fat and fruity, so always collect them when they are still fairly dry. The ivy berries in figure 7 are a good example of this early picking; most of them are very immature and even the largest is in fact only half formed as a fruit. (These seed clusters are an exception to the general rule of not pressing three-dimensional material without first trimming it.) You can see, too, in this picture the soft, brown 'Hottentot' heads of the clematis seeds. They have been picked and pressed when only half matured and the stiff stems and unusual shapes give strong angle definition to the rather square outline of this design.

Always notice the interesting coiled shapes of tendrils at this time of year. Tendrils – the twisted leaf-stalks of travellers' joy and the diminutive leaflets at the tip of a creeper such as the Virginia creeper –

Diagram 26 Contents:

Figure 9 A design of leaves and seed-heads on a dark green background surrounded by a silver-gilt, polished frame

all tend to change colour or darken in the autumn, and when placed on a pale cream or pink background will show up very well.

A striking point about design 27 is the 'skeletonised' spiky acanthus pod. In 'skeletonising' the softer, fleshier parts of a leaf or pod are removed, leaving only the pithy outline of the 'skeleton'. A lengthy, slow boiling in water will help to break down the soft parts so that they can be brushed gently away exposing the lines of white pith. (There are fuller instructions about this in the Information section.) Hydrangea florets have been 'skeletonised' and used to good effect in several of the autumn designs (see diagram 28). The lightness and fragility of this material can 'lift' a pattern in solid leaves which might otherwise appear heavy.

Autumn and harvest festivals are synonymous in many people's minds. Pressed flowers, though at first glance unlikely candidates for inclusion in church decoration, can be used here very successfully. They can never compete with the huge arrangements of fresh flowers or with the decorative piled-up patterns of fruit and vegetables, but as quiet, beautiful ornamentation on the small fabric hangings known as church furnishings they can hold their own.

Most churches will have one or two markers in the big Bible on the lectern, and these can be replaced by lengths of wide ribbon or carefully folded pieces of material decorated with pressed-flower designs. There may well be a corresponding pulpit fall which hangs

Diagram 27 Contents:
 1. Virginia creeper
 2. willow
 3. fern
 4. Virginia creeper
 5. variegated maple
 6. maple
 7. creeping buttercup
 8. clematis montana
 9. cineraria maritima
10. blackberry
11. acanthus
12. honesty
13. berries
14. hydrangea (skeletonised)
15. clematis heads
16. grass

Diagram 28 Contents:

1. creeper leaves
2. rhus leaves
3. red maple leaf
4. honesty seed-heads
5. fuchsia
6. centre of design filled with mixed hydrangea florets
7. hydrangeas 'skeletonised'
8. fuchsia

from the book rest in the pulpit, and this too will be an excellent place to have a flower 'picture'.

Always approach the priest in charge of the church before you plan any decorative work on the furnishings, and once you have obtained permission it is also sensible to contact the person who is responsible for the upkeep of the church linen as well. Church furnishings comprise not only Bible markers and pulpit falls but also altar frontals, burses and veils. It is not suggested that those associated with the altar should be decorated.

Church furnishings are made in sets in five different colourings – red, purple, green, white or gold – and each set is used according to the liturgical calendar. The ordered use of colour in these matters is something it is wise to remember when you are planning decorated markers or falls.

Harvest festival brings to mind lovely combinations of gold and browns, yellows and reds, with leaves and grasses to augment warm-coloured flowers. Seeds and seed-heads, small berries and lightly pressed 'everlasting' flowers included in your design will give extra depth to it and will echo the idea of the 'fruits of the fields' which is, after all, always the main theme of harvest decoration. Keep your design bold in colour and outline – remember the people sitting at the back of the church. Advice on how to make falls and markers can be found in the information section under church furnishings and Bible markers. (See also figure 10).

50

Figure 10 Three stages in the making of a Bible-marker. The basic
outline, marked with leaves and grasses and a very few blue flowers, has
set the style and size of the design. The next step is to complete the
outline and to continue the building up of colour. It can be seen that the
size of the small flower heads gradually increases, although in the top
and bottom of the design they are kept small. In the finished marker
more white flowers in the shape of daisies, anaphalis, honesty and cow-
parsley have lightened the clear blue of the delphiniums, clary, ceanothus
and hydrangeas, and the final flowers to be fixed into the arrangement
are a fine purple-blue anemone and two small pansies. The overall effect
is of silver and white mixed in with strong blue and this is heightened by
the white silk of the background and the shiny fringe at the bottom

Enjoy the new experience of using bright leaves and unusual material for your designs in the autumn; it is a far cry from the small delicate flowers in the spring, but nonetheless rewarding. Experiment with larger designs and patterns; try out the bigger leaves and working in grander picture frames. You may have to stand back like a painter in order to appreciate your work of art, but you will get fresh pleasure in achieving a different style of flower decoration.

Diagram 29 A big, sweeping design of autumn leaves and flowers. Deep red acer leaves, green and red hydrangeas, a blue periwinkle, some graceful fuchsias and a single pink godetia. The smallest fly-away leaves remind one of the strong winds at the end of this season

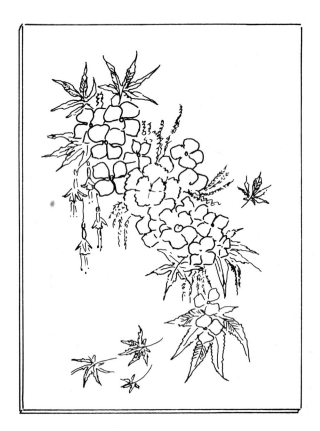

GARDEN FLOWERS FOR PRESSING – AUTUMN

English Common Name	Botanical Name	Pressing Notes
anaphalis (white) (P)	A. margaritacea	b&f Press individually and in clusters
caryopteris (blue) (Sh)	C. clandonensis	f Press whole tips of flowers
ceratostigma (blue) (Sh)	C. willmottianum	f A spectacular blue
chrysanthemum (various) (A)	C. carinatum C. coronarium C. segetum	f Hard pressing is necessary
fuchsia (various) (Sh)		f Press buds whole. Bisect flowers
golden rod (yellow) (P)	Solidago	f Single flowers or small sprays
hydrangea (blue/pink) (Sh)		f Leave some flowers to darken for late picking
Japanese anemone (pink/white) (Tb)	A. hybrida	bf Pick only freshly opened flowers
Michaelmas daisies (various) (P)	Aster	f Use only small, compact flowers
montbretia (orange/brown) (Tb)	C. × crocosmiliflora	b&f Press whole tips of stems
statice – sea lavender (various) (HHA)	S. limonium	b&f An 'everlasting' flower, dries easily

WILD FLOWERS FOR PRESSING – AUTUMN

Common English Name	Botanical Name	Pressing Notes
bell heather (P)	Erica cinerea	f Leaves fall when dry
bird's-foot trefoil (Y)	Lotus corniculatus	bfls Press small pods lightly
black medick (Y)	Medicago lupulina	fs Miniature yellow clovers
bog asphodel (Y)	Narthecium ossifragum	bfl Small leaves curve beautifully
bog heather (Pr)	Erica tetralix	f Colour will fade in old flowers
cow wheat (Y)	Melampryum pratense	fl Dries black
devil's bit scabious (B)	Succisa pratensis	bf Colour a little fugitive
fat hen (G)	Chenopodium album	fl Flowers grey spikes
fennel (Y)	Foeniculum vulgare	bf Florets press very well
feverfew (W)	Tanacetum parthenium	f Florets retain whiteness
field scabious (B)	Knautia arvensis	f Old flowers will fade in press
fleabane (Y)	Pulicaria dysenterica	f Press buds in profile as well
grass of parnassus (W)	Parnassia palustris	f Flowers best left growing unless prolific
herb Robert (P)	Geranium robertianum	fls Leaves colour well
honeysuckle (Cr)	Lonicera periclymenum	f Pick only the young flowers
ling heather (Pr)	Calluna vulgaris	f Easy to press in all stages
mallow (Pr)	Calluna vulgaris	f Press double quantity – dries transparent
milkwort (B/W/P)	Polygala vulgaris	bf Beautiful blue. Pick sparingly
montbretia (O)	Crocosmia × crocosmiaflora	bf Tips of flowering stems only

mugwort (G)	*Artemisia vulgaris*	bfl Silver/green leaves are unusual
nipplewort (Y)	*Lapsana communis*	bf Round buds dry black
rosebay willowherb (Pr)	*Epilobium augustifolium*	bf Single flowers and the spike of buds
sea lavender (Pr & W)	*Limonium vulgare*	f Very easy and quick to dry
St John's wort (Y)	*Hypericum perforatum*	f Separate flowers and buds
tansy (Y)	*Tenacetum vulgare*	bf Bright yellow is retained. Press hard
vetch (P)	*Vicia sepium*	f ten Press small pods and tendrils too
water mint (P)	*Mentha aquatica*	b Choose flowers with young leaves
white bryony (G)	*Bryonia dioica*	fl ten Press flowers carefully
wild pansy (Pr)	*Viola tricolor*	bfl Very easy to press. Trim stem
yarrow (W, occ.P)	*Achillea millefolium*	fl Pink and white. Very useful

LEAVES FOR PRESSING – AUTUMN

Brown

azalea (Sh)   epimedium (P)
beech (T)   hawthorn (T)
bracken (F)   sycamore (T)
Clematis montana (Cl)

Yellow

ginkgo (T)
hawthorn (T)
Robinia pseudoacacia (T)
willow (T)

Green

ferns (F)
ivy (Cl)
holly (T)
lawsoniana (T)

Grey

Alchemilla alpina (P)   *Santolina chamaecyparissus* (Sh)
Cineraria maritima (Sh)   *Senecio greyii* (Sh)
Potentilla anserina (W)

Two-coloured

epimedium (P)
tiarella (P)

Seedheads

agapanthus pods   pampas
clematis   rosebay willowherb
herb Robert   traveller's joy
honesty   umbelliferae
ivy   vetch pods

4 Winter

Winter. Cold winds and snow, fog and frost. A desire to sit by the fire or cuddle a mug of coffee in the warm kitchen, and a determination at all costs to keep out of the garden. Thoughts on the subject of flowers are channelled into the order pages of nurserymen's magazines, new vistas are imagined and unloved corners of your garden are replanned. Garden inspection at this time of year is made only too often through the window and praise of it will be limited to its tidiness. When the pale sun shines and you venture out of doors, you will find that nearly all your old friends in the flower beds are asleep and the stalks cut back, and the only leaves in evidence are dry, loose ones scattered about into corners by the eddying wind. There are a very few stalwarts still showing leaf – the holly and the ivy, immortalised for every winter by the carol, the coniferous trees and some variegated shrubs. There may be berries on the pyracantha, *Skimmia japonica* and cotoneaster, and these will be bright and cheerful; the winter-flowering viburnum and the *Hamamelis mollis* whose tiny flowers cling close to the branches will comfort us too, but by and large there are few common garden plants in December, January and early February that show much inclination to burst into bloom.

Perhaps it should come as no surprise that the bravest of the early British flowers are usually yellow. What little sun there is must feel doubly welcomed by finding its own cheerful gold reflected in the winter aconite, the winter jasmine and the early coltsfoot and celandine, which all show their golden flowers at the most cold and inhospitable times.

At this time of the year flowers in the house take on a different look. The summer vases are replaced by dried arrangements or by expensive chrysanthemums grown under glass, and the pot plants take over and become the first contenders for our attention. The ability to strike up a working relationship with your first poinsettia is all important now. When and how to water the foreigner is vital. Take your eye off it for half a day, give it more to drink than it wants, keep it thirsty for half an hour, forget to turn its foliage towards the window and . . . whoosh! Down fall the leaves and you have, instead of the great burgeoning tropical visitor, miserable bunches of red tufts on bare spikes to advertise your neglect and incompetence.

Finding flowers to press in the winter is obviously going to be a much harder task than at any other time of the year, but for the

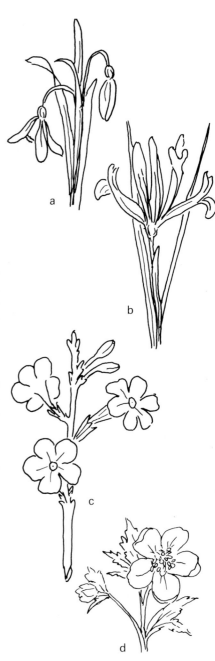

Diagram 30
a. snowdrop
b. iris reticulata
c. winter jasmine
d. hellebore

55

Diagram 31
a. silver lace
b. *Peris biavrita*
c. button fern

Diagram 32 This is a design composed almost entirely of ferns grown indoors in the winter months. The plain wooden frame is 32cm (12½in) square and the colour is all-greens and creams with, here and there, a touch of deep pink in the young fronds of *Adiantum pubescens*. In the centre there are pieces of *Adiantum grossum* which have pressed beautifully, retaining their deep fresh green. Some of the maidenhair leaves have been laid with the reverse sides showing and the half-formed spores can be seen. A very modest leaf of the 'parlour palm' lies on the right-hand side of the design; this is the only stanger in this family of ferns. Contents: *Adiantum fragrans – Pellaea rotundifolia – Pteris cretica albolineata – Adiantum grossum – Pteris arguta – Pteris roweri – Adiantum pubescens – Polystichum setigerum – Neanthe bella*

purpose of this chapter we will pretend that you have received a flower press as a Christmas present and want to start pressing flowers and leaves as soon as you can. The warm sun of April and gentle drifts of spring flowers seem a long way away and you must make the best use of what little there is in the way of winter-growing plants. Out of doors there may well be very few indeed; continual rain, cold winds, frost and snow will subdue and spoil most growing things – even the indomitable three, the ivy, groundsel and shepherd's purse, which are always listed in botany books as 'growing/flowering period, January to December', will be temporarily defeated. Indoors, however, it is a different story; there are the pot plants grown by nurserymen in greenhouses, and you will find in these often flamboyant plants a new and alternative source of material for your press. They fall into three main groups: ferns, a number of what are known today as 'foliage' house plants, and the more traditional flowering plants. If you intend to start a small collection of them to provide leaves for pressing, then a simple book on the general care of all indoor plants is a sensible addition to your shelf of gardening books.

Fashion has ordained that ferns can return to our houses; much loved by our Victorian great-grandparents, they are now 'in', and their fresh greenery adorns many offices, hotels and smart reception areas (diagram 31). Maidenhair, *Adiantum fragrans, Pteris arguta* and *roweri*, the button fern, *Pellaea rotundifolia* and even those dissolute piles of fronds in the Nepholepis group are all propagated in greenhouses commercially. Generally speaking, ferns are inexpensive and are worthwhile plants to welcome into one's home; for a modest

amount you can achieve a fine tray full of different varieties and if you add to this the fact that they will press well, then you can start buying straight away.

We have used ferns in two of our winter pictures to show that they can be used very successfully when they have been pressed (diagram 32). The varieties we have used dry very easily and quickly in the press and the bright green is retained in the wafer-thin fronds. You will, amongst others, see *Adiantum fragrans* and *pubescens*, the *Pteris cretica* and *arguta*, the little *Pellaea rotundafolia* and even a small leaf of *Neanthe bella* or 'parlour palm'. All these leaves with their delicate fronds should be cut cleanly from the plant and laid flat on to the blotting paper where they will dry, when tightly pressed, in a few weeks. In the case of *Adiantum grossum* and *Pteris roweri* you will have to take extra care when you are putting them into the press, since they have curly fronds which thicken up the shape of the leaf; pressed successfully, however, they should provide useful – if slightly thicker – material for your fern pictures, and both these ferns have been included in the design and help to create a more substantial centre.

Minute fern fronds photographed in figure 11 have been arranged in two different ways and fixed down on to cream card to illustrate the ease with which you can arrive at a fresh, simple design in ferns alone, using only their flowing shape to guide you. There are drawings too of common ferns (diagrams 31 and 32) which you are likely to find in shops and nurseries and we have given both the Latin and the common English name. All the ones illustrated are usually easy to press and this basic choice will help you when you are buying for the first time.

Ferns and delicate cinerarias are often found flourishing in our centrally heated houses. In figure 12 we have combined the fronds of some ferns with six different coloured cineraria flower heads, and together they give a surprisingly fresh winter picture.

There is a wonderful variety of leaves in the 'foliage' houseplants, ranging from the green and white dracaenas and small fittonias to the old umbrella-shaped leaves of heptapleurum, and many of them will give you foliage to press which is both unusual and amusing (diagram 33). They will take more room in the press than summer leaves, not only because they are often large; they are also frequently thick, holding a lot of moisture, and require a good expanse of fresh blotting paper to be dried in. They are sometimes very brightly coloured indeed; red, yellow, cream, white or even purple combining with every shade of green, in spots, stripes or blotches and other exotic colour mixes. It is usually worth experimenting and pressing one or two of these leaves; many of them will fade but some will retain a little of their former brightness and remain a pleasant echo of their true selves.

There are some leaves with two, or even three bright shades in them which will fade so badly that they can never be pressed for reasons of colour alone. You must instead take the shape of the leaf as the most important factor. Imagine it faded to a desert fawn and laid

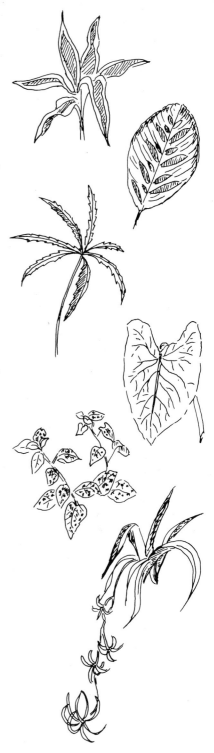

Diagram 33 Plant leaves

Figure 11 Greetings cards decorated with pressed ferns. The cream card measures 15cm (6in) by 10cm (4in) and the very small fronds are fixed firmly down with minute touches of adhesive. The shade variation between the different greens is very attractive

on a white background. If the shape would still be interesting, graceful, delicate or even bizarre, then press it; the change in the colour, even the total loss of the original pattern will not concern you. Making a 'flower' picture using this type of material is quite different from using pressed flowers and leaves picked at other times of the year. Shape and texture now dictate the starting-point for your designs. The outline of the leaves with their wonderful variety of sharp or rounded points and smooth or jagged edges will quickly give you inspiration. The building up of the differing colour shades, which are often small and subtle, is also very demanding and exciting to do.

The winter colour plate is devoted solely to these leaves. Its size, 53cm (21in) in height and 45cm (18in) across, will demonstrate how,

58

Figure 12 The modern frame is quite large and measures 30cm (12in) across and 36cm (14in) from top to bottom. There is plenty of plain white background around the light design of ferns and cinerarias and this emphasises its delicacy. Pteris, adiantum and pellaea fronds give the design a flowing shape and the soft colours of the cinerarias tone in with each other. All these have been picked and pressed during the winter months. Contents: *Adiantum fragrans – Pteris arguta – pteris roweri – Pteris cretica albolineata – Pallaea rotundifolia – Polystichum setigerum –* cinerarias

when working with this type of pressed material, you must enlarge both your ideas and the accompanying frames. There is a detail drawing of the picture in diagram 34.

The centre point of the picture is held in quite a dramatic manner by two heads of *Anthurium andreanum*, the 'wax flower'. The spikes of peperomia flower heads and the green and white stripes of the narrow grass *Acorus gramineus* give a sharpness to the top of the design, while the lovely dark green circles of both 'ivy' and 'water-melon' peperomia are a most satisfying contrast at the base. The whole of the centre is made interesting to the eye because of the differing leaf shapes and the subtlety of their colours. Some of them, like the striking green and cream striped *Aphelandra squarrosa*, have kept their colours, while others, like the single leaf of *Ananeas bracteatus striatus*, have faded to cream, but the rough saw-edge of this leaf still gives a sharp definition to the graceful lines which flow outwards. It should be remembered that a pale, neutral background – of cream or fawn perhaps – will never be in danger of overpowering the soft, almost faded tints of these leaves. You are aiming at an accentuation of the extraordinary outline some of them present. There is a list in the section on 'Winter Plants for Pressing'.

Diagram 34 Design of leaves from indoor 'foliage' plants

60

Hot-house succulents and cacti are bad candidates for your press; they have a very high water retention and little 'skeleton' to retain an interesting shape when they have dried.

The third group of winter hot-house plants which may provide useful material for pressing contains the true, forced 'flowering' plants. The main difficulty about using these flower heads is that in the very nature of their restricted winter flowering, one is reluctant to pick them! General advice, which is given in the information section, about the suitability of different flower types for pressing applies to these as well. Begonias, cyclamen and all the St Paulia group are much too 'fleshy' and impossible to dry well. Gardenias and orchids too will be disappointing. The shape of calceolarias, gloxinias and many others is against them, and it is advisable to limit pressing to those with 'open' faces. The campanulas, cinerarias and the primula family are excellent. A surprisingly good flower to press is the well known 'Cape primrose', *Streptocarpus hybridus*; the beautiful blue is nearly always preserved, and a little judicious trimming of the long, pale part at the back of the flower will ensure that it does not crumple.

Although some of the rarer specimens of hot-house plants can be expensive to buy, by far the majority that you find in your local shop should be reasonably priced. All you need for pressing are a very few leaves from a single plant and you will be able to start your own basic collection without an enormous outlay. (You can add to it by 'begging' a few leaves from a friend – a small group of 'flower pressing' devotees can help each other greatly with 'swops'!)

Very early in the year the shops will offer imported flowers for sale. Mimosa and chinchincherees, *Euphorbia fulgens* and narcissus are all worth pressing and they will give you added variety for your winter pictures. Beware of mimosa leaves, the tiny leaflets tend to drop when they are dry.

As soon as the snow melts and the frosts seem to be lessening you will find that a surreptitious change has taken place in the garden. Even though it is still cold and wintry you will notice that the spikes of the daffodils are now several inches up above the ground, a few hellebores are uncurling their green heads and hidden behind large leaves a pink bergenia flower is open. After a couple of weeks of mild weather a few snowdrops and iris stylosa come out to join the winter flowering ericas and already (if you can bear to pick them) you will have sufficient flowers to make a small winter picture. Remember to press too the yellow stars from the winter jasmine, and you may well find that there are flowers on the daphne and the early flowering viburnum.

Diagram 35 shows a small picture made from these early flowers designed especially for a child's bedroom. The back of the plain wood frame is secured by four spring clips so that the flower design can be easily changed. The 'winter' ones could be replaced by 'summer' holiday ones, picked and pressed perhaps by the owner of the bedroom. Our wintery flowers are snowdrops, white heather, helle-

bores, a single iris head and some pink bergenia, and they are mounted on a piece of sugar-pink cotton and bordered by modest pink buds.

We have made two other true winter pictures. Diagrams 36 and 37 and the black and white photographs (figures 13 and 14) show how attractive they can be. The colours in the first picture, diagram 26, are white, creams and greens and they are laid on a dark green background. There are two complete snowdrop plants – roots and all – on the left of the picture and one is again surprised by the diminutive size of these plants which choose to flower at such inhospitable times. The second design, diagram 37, is a symbolic winter picture made mainly from plant material picked during the three coldest months – the stark white and brown is very evocative of this time of year when all the colour has gone from the garden and all the flowers have died. You will find late grasses still growing in sheltered places in late November and early December, also the garden honesty and the seed-heads and the brown thistles in the countryside. Then you can add the late summer grasses from your store and they will add interest and graceful line to the sparse winter material.

The flower designs which illustrate this winter section fall into two categories: there are those which are made from pressed material that has been picked only during the cold months of December, January and February, while the others are decorated with designs made from flowers collected throughout the year. This second group, which is shown in the colour illustration on the back jacket, would make ideal Christmas presents. These are much brighter in colour and perhaps more frivolous in style; they are pretty, highly-decorated things that give pleasure as gifts at this time of year. Cards, book-markers, table-mats, gift tags and calendars, they are all excellent articles for your

Figure 13 A dark background to a winter picture. The colours are limited to white and shades of green. The flowers of the snowdrops and the heather stand out from the cluster of pale hellebores and honesty. The two small florets of 'skeletonised' hydrangea lighten the effect. The picture measures 22cm (8½in) by 27cm (10½in) and the frame is black with a gold-coloured recessed line around it. Contents: hellebores, both *niger* and *corsicus* – honesty – snowdrops – ivy – heather

Diagram 36 Snowdrops, hellebores, honesty, ivy and heather on dark green

Diagram 37 Dark seeds, pale grasses, tendrils and dry thistles silhouetted

63

Figure 14 An attractive wintry-looking picture. White, browns and creams studded with dark seeds. Grasses and fly-away seed-heads, a curly tendril and thistles make this an unusual study and the dead white background suggests frosty days. The picture is small and measures 22cm (8½in) by 27cm (10½in). Contents: grasses – seed-heads – thistles – honesty – willow-herb – tendril – and 'skeletonised' acanthus and hydrangea

pressed flower decoration, each thing made to suit the recipient, and thus intrinsically personal 'matching up' of colour and flowers can give great pleasure to both sides. Nothing is more interesting than to create a little picture, for example, that is destined to hang in a specific place and to give pleasure to one particular person.

We have crowded together this Christmas collection of inexpensive presents which epitomise the way in which you can use your pressed flowers. Keep your designs simple and bright – most of these things will be used and enjoyed for a relatively short time and will then spoil or fade and be thrown away. Use bright colours and dramatic contrasts – they are cheerful reminders of summer days. At the top of our illustration we have a beautiful picture made from flowers collected throughout the year. It is full of colour and variety and has the charming conceit of a 'vase' made from tulip petals, from which everything springs upwards. The frame is wide and old in character and sets off the bright group of flowers and foliage. Christmastide in your church is a time of great festival and the church furnishings will be of either white, gold or red. We have made a wide 'bible marker' and put it among our Christmas things. It is bright and would be effective even from some distance away. The silver and white 'swag' is in strong contrast to the scarlet satin with its matching fringe.

Table-mats are extremely welcome presents (diagram 38). Made from either good quality glass with the edges sanded smooth, or from thick clear perspex, they can have the flowers stuck on to thin hardboard backings and the two surfaces can be pinched together – either glued tightly or bonded with heavy-duty tape which can be finally masked by braid. Detailed instructions for making mats similar to these can be found in the Information section.

Bookmarkers can be made from a great number of materials: card, thick paper, leather, parchment or almost any cloth provided it is sufficiently well stiffened for you to fix the pressed flowers on to it (diagram 39a). The markers can be covered with a protective plastic film covering if you wish, or 'heat sealed', and this will prevent damage to the delicate petals.

Gift tags and calendars are made in the same way as Christmas cards except for the difference in the size of the background card (diagram 39b). Some of the coloured tags in the picture on the back jacket have gold flowers on them, and they can be made to complement similarly coloured Christmas cards. The dark brown one in the photograph is made like this, being decorated with dried seeds, flowers and leaves which have been made independently, sprayed with gold and then stuck on to the card.

The two calendars illustrated on the back jacket have been made with pressed flower arrangements fixed into card mounts. Such cards can be covered with protective skins of plastic to safeguard the flowers; the larger of the two illustrates the use of heat sealing, which has given the card a very tough and practically invisible coating.

Diagram 38a Circular mat measuring 23cm (9in). Flowers used include green hellebore, buttercups and orange potentilla, with various leaves on a green silk base. Blackberry and Virginia creeper leaves add extra colour

Diagram 38b A mat 20cm (8in) in diameter. The flowers are fixed in a crescent design and include green hydrangea flowers and crimson primulas, with a single astrantia in the centre. Ferns and alchemilla leaves show up well against a cream background

c

d

a

b

Diagram 39 a. Book-marker of ribbon (3.5cm [1½in] wide) (3.5 × 14cm [1½ × 7in] wide) b. Diminutive flowers decorate a card and gift tag (5 × 6.3cm [2 × 2½in]) c. A calendar made on card fixed to a mount (32.5 × 20cm [13 × 8in]) d. Pressed flowers fixed with adhesive to a card base. The arrangement has been covered with Transpaseal to protect it (14 × 10cm [5½ × 4in])

You will get a great deal of enjoyment when you are decorating these small Christmas things – they are fun to make, requiring both your ingenuity and artistry. People are usually interested in the flowers that you have used and try to identify them; a note of them, neatly writtten on the back of the calendar or card, giving either the 'country' names or the Latin ones, will be much appreciated.

Christmas is over, it is the end of the year and all four seasons and their flowers have gone by. Each season has been very different from the others, and every time there has been a distinct change in the pattern of flowering plants you have been able to press and create new flower pictures. They will always remind you of the four seasons of natural beauty that are completed with the ending of every year.

GARDEN FLOWERS FOR PRESSING – WINTER

Common English Name	Botanical Name	Pressing Notes
bergenia (various) (P)		bf Pick young flowers; old ones fade
crocus (various) (Bb)		f Dries rather transparent. Mount or use two
daphne (pink) (Sh)	D. mezereum	f Single pink flowers
garrya (grey–green) (Sh)	G. elliptica	f Long catkins
heather (pink, white, red) (Sh)	Erica carnea	fl Leaflets drop off when dry
hellebores (P)	H. atrorubens (pink/purple) H. corsicus (green) H. niger (the Christmas rose)	bfl All press well. With old flowers remove pistil and press separately
hepatica (various) (P)	Anemone hepatica	f Delicate flowers. Handle carefully when dry
iris (purple) (Tb)	I. stylosa	f Difficult. The deep colour is fugitive
mahonia (yellow) (Sh)	M. japonica	fl Long tails of yellow flowers often drying to grey
primula (various) (P)		bfl Most primulas press very well and retain colour
snowdrop (white) (Bb)	Galanthus nivalis	bfl There are several varieties which all press well
viburnum (cream/white) (Sh)	V. fragrans V. tinus (Lauristinus)	f Press florets singly
winter jasmine (Sh)	J. nudiflorum	bf Trim away the back corolla tube a little before pressing

WILD FLOWERS FOR PRESSING – WINTER

Except for groundsel and shepherd's purse there are no true wild
flowers in bloom during the cold winter months. The odd late-
flowering umbelliferae can be found occasionally until the frosts
start, and at the end of winter in well-sheltered western areas,
small spring flowers are sometimes deceived into opening a single
flower in a mild January or February.

LEAVES FOR PRESSING – WINTER

Chrysanthemum haradjanii
hellebore
ivy
snowdrop

FERNS FOR PRESSING – WINTER

Adiantum fragrans
Adiantum grossum
Adiantum pubescens
Neanthe bella
Nephrolepis exaltata
Nephrolepis exaltata bostoniensis
Nephrolepis exaltata 'fluffy ruffles'
Pellaea rotundifolia
Polystichum setigerum
Pteris arguta
Pteris cretica albolineata
Pteris cretica cristata
Pteris ensiformis victoriae
Pteris roweri

FOLIAGE PLANTS FOR PRESSING – WINTER

Acorus gramineus – sweet flat
Ananas bracteatus striatus
Ananas comosus variegatus – ivory pineapple
Anthurium andreanum – wax flower
Anthurium scherzerianum – flamingo flower
Aphelandra squarrosa – zebra plant
Asparagus meyeri – plume asparagus
Caladium bicolour candidum
Calathea mackoyona – peacock plant
Carex japonica – sedge
Cyperus papyrus
Fittonia argyroneura – snakeskin plant
Fittonia verschaffeltii – red-veined fittonia
Hemigraphis colorata – red ivy
Heptapleurum arboricola – umbrella plant
Maranta tricolor
Pellaea rotundifolia – button fern
Peperomia argyreia – watermelon peperomia
Peperomia hederaefolia – ivy peperomia
Spathiphyllum – peace lily
Syngonium podophyllum
Tradescantia family – wandering Jews

3. Three autumn pictures made with beautiful leaves, berries and seed-heads.
There are few flowers here but nevertheless they are still full of bright colour

4. A large, black and gold frame surrounds a strong, effective design of coloured leaves laid on a cream background. The leaves are all from 'foliage' house plants grown indoors and picked in the early months of the year. Contents include:-
Aphelandra squarrosa – Maranta tricolor – Ananas – Tradescantia – Asparagus meyeri – Peperomia hederaefolia and *argyeria – Pellaea rotundifolia – Heptapleurum – Dracaena godseffiana – Caladium – Fittonia argyroneura – Anthurium andreanum – Hemigraphis colorata – Cyperus papyrus – Spathiphyllum* and flowers from peperomia

Information Section

Adhesive Keep a variety of different adhesives in stock. Glues and gums are usually sold with instructions for use and information about which substances they will bond together. The ubiquitous 'Copydex' and similar adhesives are easy to use; they dry clear and are excellent for fixing in place fragile materials such as pressed flowers, the edges of fine cottons, silks and papers. The even milder 'roll on' fixatives such as 'Pritt Stick' are good for holding paper and card together. Platignum 'Spot Stick' which, as its name suggests, releases a tiny spot of gum at a time, is invaluable when you are mounting or repairing flowers. Stronger glues such as 'Bostic', household gums and 'Araldite' are essential for frame repairs. A golden rule to be observed when you are using any type of adhesive: always use the minimum – a smear instead of a splodge!

Albums Update the Victorian idea of compiling an album of pressed flowers. Put your holiday flowers into a small photograph album (diagram 40) and keep on adding a fresh design after every holiday and you will soon have a beautiful momento. You will need the type of album that has plain card pages with a transparent, self-adhesive film attached – one measuring 23cm (9in) square will be ideal. Have ready your leaves and chosen pressed flowers, peel back the film of a page and lay the flowers on to the card, arrange them carefully until you have achieved the effect you want and then replace the plastic film. The flowers will be held safely in place and the book, when closed, will protect your work. A small album measuring 23cm (9in) square will not cost very much and can be bought from most good stationers and booksellers.

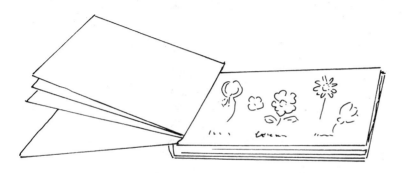

Diagram 40 A small album containing holiday flowers

Backgrounds It is useful to have a selection of coloured card handy to use as sample background shades when you are planning a picture. Shop around both locally and in the big towns and build up a collection; art and craft shops and good stationers as well as specialist paper shops should be able to help you. In the same way you should collect samples of fabrics in creams, browns, greens etc of differing shades and types of cloth. Experimenting with these will help you to decide on the balance of colour and surface texture between frame, background and flower design. Try out different effects with your samples at home and then buy, eventually, with greater confidence. Remember that 'sympathetic' colours for most dried flowers are white, cream, greens, greys and browns. Difficult colours are yellows, blues and purples. Don't be frightened by the idea of black or scarlet.

Paper Backgrounds can be of paper and cards of all sorts. The most expensive varieties are not necessarily the best, although very cheap, thin paper will be unsatisfactory. Use a guillotine for cutting both paper and card – much easier than scissors.

Fabrics Cottons, silks, linens, terylene and many other 'man-made' fibres, lining fabrics and felts – any of these materials can make excellent backgrounds when in keeping with the frame and size of flower design. Search in both furnishing and dress fabric shops. (See 'Fabrics' for further advice.)

Bible Makers in churches. These can be made from a long narrow piece of material, lined and folded at one end, decorated with a design of pressed flowers (diagrams 41 and 42). Most churches have a fine Bible on a lectern or reading desk and at festival time when the church is decorated with flowers and leaves, a pair of markers or even a single marker laid through the pages and allowed to hang down in front of the lectern can add to the overall beauty of the church. The length and width of a marker is dependent on the size and height of the Bible on its lectern – it is advisable not to make it too narrow or an effective display of pressed flowers will be difficult to achieve. A pulled self-fringe is very suitable. The colour of the marker and the flowers should be chosen with two things in mind; the colour of the church furnishings to be used during the festival and the colour of the fresh flowers to be arranged near the lectern. The design of the flowers must be effective from a distance – remember the congregation sitting far back in the church as well as those close to. The flowers should be chosen from your store and laid loose on the marker base – use tweezers always when handling pressed flowers – and only when the design is completed to your satisfaction should the flowers be lifted, touched lightly with adhesive on the back and then replaced on the material. (Instructions for fixing down flowers is described in further detail under 'Fixed Method' (See also figure 10).

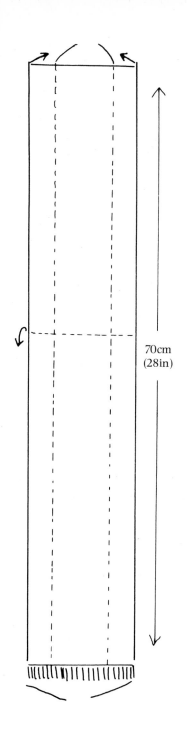

70cm
(28in)

Diagram 41 Bible marker, material cut to size. 'Tacking' threads show the two fold lines. (Note: fringe has already been pulled)

Diagram 42 Marker completed with flower decoration in bold colours (40 × 8cm [16 × 3in])

Blotting Paper The good, old-fashioned, white blotting paper is unbeatable for use in pressing and drying flowers. Each large sheet can be folded and halved down to 44cm by 29cm (17½in by 11½in) or reduced even further if you are using a very small press, and the sheets can be used over and over again. (We have veteran pages still in use which are dated back to the early sixties!) Buy blotting paper in bulk if you can; a quire of 24 sheets is the minimum wholesale quantity and it is cheaper than buying small packets at a time. It is possible to buy a few sheets of blotting paper at a reasonable price, but they are often tightly rolled, it takes time and patience to flatten them satisfactorily and flowers will slide about on a curving surface. The quality of these inexpensive sheets can be poor, which means that they tear easily and will have to be replaced soon. It should be appreciated that if you are going to press enough flowers to make pictures throughout the year, you will need a large amount of blotting paper.

Book-markers A simple strip of ribbon, card or folded silk ornamented with pressed flowers will make an attractive marker for a book and an ideal small gift. Pressed flowers are fragile and rough treatment will damage them, but a book-marker allowed to lie between the pages of a book and moved with a modicum of care can last for a long time. Flower material used for markers must be fixed down securely, especially at the loose tips of petals and leaves. It is possible to cover book-markers with a thin plastic film; this can either be cut flush with the edges of the marker and stuck down with a minute strip of adhesive down each side or it can be folded neatly behind the marker, the edges hidden underneath a second layer of material. This will protect the flower design, the only disadvantage being that it can look a little shiny. Book-markers can be covered with plastic film and subjected to 'heat-sealing'. This can be an excellent way of overcoming their fragility (See 'Heat-sealing').

Botanical Pictures Some plants have attractive colour and shape in both flowers and leaves. Even their buds, seed-heads and the manner of growth may be eminently decorative and when this natural beauty is combined with good pressing qualities one need go no further in

Diagram 43 Primroses

72

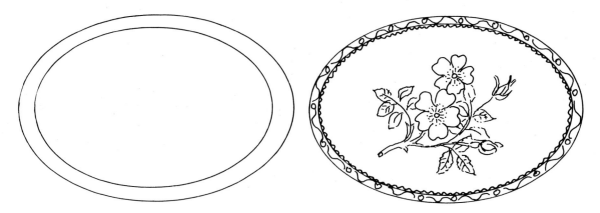

Diagram 44 Wild roses

planning a flower picture (diagram 43). Press flowers from unusual angles, full face and in profile, in tight bud and half out, remembering the small leaves and a substantial piece of stalk. Small single climbing roses, traveller's joy and small clematis, snowdrop and passion flowers, are some of the plants which will enjoy having a picture to themselves (diagram 44). Wild flower enthusiasts also will get pleasure from making a flower design which shows every aspect of growth in a more humble flower such as a daisy, a violet or even the ubiquitous stinging nettle! The strawberries in the small spring colour picture and the celandine in diagram 3 illustrate this type of picture.

Buds Always consider picking and pressing a few buds when you gather the fully opened flowers (see diagram 45). Sometimes the shape alone is charming, as in the poppy and the tall bocconia, but often the colour of the emerging petals is deeper than it is in the matured bloom and this can be very useful in a design. The buds of apple blossom, early prunus and montbretia are excellent examples of this. When pressing thick buds it may be advisable to bisect them from top down through to the stalk and then to lay both halves on the sheet of blotting paper. Not only do thick buds tend to get mould, they also loose their shape and shrivel. By dividing them you will not only get success – you will also get two for the price of one! Remember too that

Diagram 45 Buds
a. comfrey
b. poppy
c. rose
d. larkspur
e. montbretia

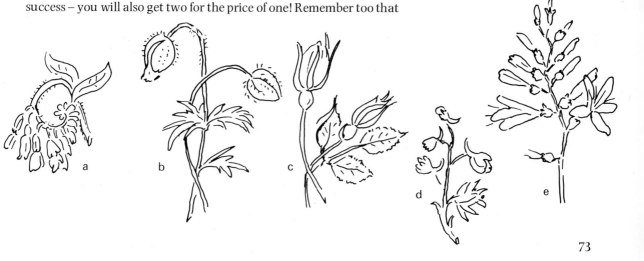

73

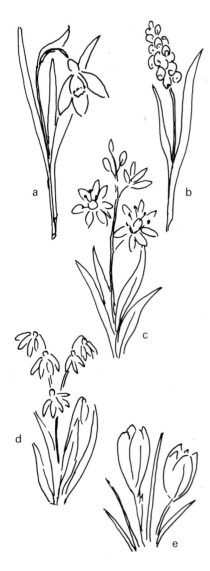

small clusters of buds, such as deutzia and the common traveller's joy, often press very well. The pearl-like buds of exochorda and those of elderflower, which dry dark brown, are both particularly useful in pictures.

Bulbs Bulbs which produce flowers in early spring (see diagram 46) are particularly useful for flower pressing; these little flowers are invariably the first out after the dead months of the winter. Fortunately the flowers often press very well and the following short list includes some old favourites:

allium	grape hyacinth	scilla
Anemone blanda	*Lily pyrenaicum*	snowdrop
anemone	narcissus (miniature)	'star of Bethlehem'
chionodoxa	martagon lily	tulips (miniature)

Large flowers such as tulips and daffodils, hyacinths and bluebells as well as the big lilies are all very unrewarding to press, since both their shape and their size are against them. The miniature daffodils, narcissi, tulips and lilies will press satisfactorily but the first should have the trumpet either half-slashed and turned sideways or pressed separately, the central frill of a narcissus must be 'nicked' with scissors in places and pressed flat, while the tulips and lilies should be bisected with a razor blade or sharp knife and the two halves pressed independently. Small irises will press but are unreliable; their triangular shape is against them, and the blue varieties tend to fade.

Card An essential element in making pressed flower pictures because card makes an admirable base upon which to place your flower design. Points to remember when choosing card are surface absorbency – any writing or border inking will be ruined by the ink running into the fibres of the card; and surface shine – a very highly polished card may not enhance the simple flowers. The cost too has to be considered carefully; although the cost of a sheet of card may not be very high you will have to buy the whole sheet even though you may

Diagram 46
a. snowdrop
b. grape hyacinth
c. chionodoxa
d. scilla
e. crocus
f. narcissus
g. *Tulip kaufmannia*
h. martagon lily

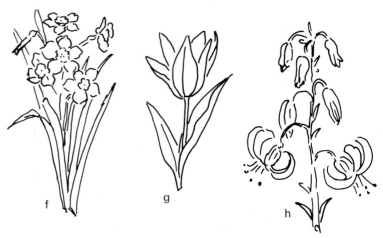

74

only require a small piece a few inches square! Hunt around, you will find card in good stationers and art and craft shops – occasionally you will be able to buy small postcard-sized pieces of coloured card, but it is unlikely that you will achieve this outside London. Don't be afraid of buying inexpensive card; sometimes the rough texture of the surface and the broken colour can be an attractive background for pressed flowers. There is no standard size for card.

Cards For Christmas, Easter, birthdays, anniversaries and other occasions cards decorated with pressed flowers invariably give great pleasure to the recipient. Each card having been individually designed and made, they become essentially small personal gifts and may well be kept and framed instead of being consigned to the wastepaper basket. They can be made of card or of good quality paper; you can draw or ink a border just inside the outside edge of the card, or draw a circle on the card of any colour you like, and stick your flowers in the centre. Use your imagination when you are doing the design for a card, and experiment with different effects. Avoid very heavy, overcrowded designs. There are firms which specialise in plain cards ideal for mounting pressed flowers. (See list of stockists at end of book.)

Church Furnishing It is advisable to understand the meaning of the word 'furnishings' and to appreciate the colour changes and their significance before you offer to replace any of them with ones decorated with pressed flower designs. Flower festivals in churches are very popular, and the inclusion of pressed-flower decoration on pulpit and lectern falls and on Bible markers can add to the general beauty of the church. Despite their modest size and soft colouring they can hold their own with the great vases and 'swags' of fresh flowers. Always ask permission of the priest in charge, and it is sensible to liaise with the member of the church who is responsible for the altar linen and frontals. Church furnishings comprise altar frontals, burses and veils, all of which are connected with the altar, pulpit and lectern falls, Bible markers and covers. It is suggested that only the falls and the markers are really suitable for replacement by specially made ones decorated with pressed flower designs. Church furnishings are made in sets of one colour, either green, red, purple, white or gold, and each colour is used at the proper time in the church's calendar.

Collars These are made from one or two layers of blotting paper, usually not more than a few inches square, with a small hole cut in them so that they can be placed easily round the stem of a thick flower when it is put into press (diagram 47). A 'collar' can be useful when pressing daisy-type flowers such as cineraria, chrysanthemums and other flowers with a solid calyx thick in proportion to the petals. A single layer 'collar' will help to guard against failure or petal-curl in many other flowers which are awkward to press.

Diagram 47 A daisy-shaped flower requiring a 'collar' during pressing

Collecting Flowers for Pressing Flowers for pressing should be picked when they are dry and freshly out (diagram 48). They must be carried carefully so that they are not damaged, preferably in a small sealed container or a little plastic bag, and put as quickly as possible into the press. When you are travelling take a very small lightweight press with you – this is essential in very hot weather when flowers wilt in a short time. Never pick more flowers than you need, and never pick more than one or two from a single plant; remember that every flower left on the plant turns into the seed-head which will ensure more blooms next year. Remember the leaves, the buds and tendrils and the occasional seed-head if it is not too thick to press. Some plants which have very unprepossessing flowers have beautiful foliage – 'silverweed', *Potentilla anserina*, is a good example. Three rules to follow:

Never pick in the rain.
Never pick old flowers and leaves.
Never waste a flower.

Diagram 48 A page of August flowers ready for pressing. The flowers were picked on a country walk and include daisies, woody nightshade, thyme, mint, trefoil, polygonum, *Potentilla anserina* and other leaves

Colour The success of a pressed-flower design is obviously greatly dependent upon colour – the colours of the flowers in the design itself and also the overall balance of colour between the frame, the background and the flower design. Considerable thought should be given to these two aspects of picture-making, because the ultimate effect of your artistic effort is governed by the choice of colour. There can be a subtle blending of shades or there can be a direct contrast between, say, a gold frame, a dark chocolate background, and white flowers or cream grasses. Experiment with colour – nature provides you with a wonderful palette. Remember that the colour in flowers often changes during drying and pressing. Some white flowers will dry cream, while a lot of red ones will get darker. Blue petals tend to fade, and there are some which change colour completely. Pale yellow or white flowers are useful 'mixing' colours for a design where you want to have a full herbaceous border! Remember too that pressed flowers will naturally fade a little over the years, so be careful that your frames and backgrounds are not too bright in shade, or they may appear overpowering in a few years' time. The easiest colours for background are creams and ivories, the very dark shades coming a good second.

Design The colour, line, shape and style of a design are all interwoven in a flower picture, and can be considered separately when you are planning a picture; above all there must be harmony between flowers, background and frame.

Colour The colour range in pressed flowers and leaves is very wide. It can range from the almost black stars of veratrum and dark brown buds of elderflower to the palest pinks, creams and the pristine white of xeranthemum. Experimenting with different colours and shades is a continuing delight, and it is impossible to lay down rules for colour combination because so often the most satisfying is purely a matter of personal preference. Beware of very bright colours scattered wildly among very pale ones – a graduation of shades is more attractive and easily pleasing to the eye. Use colour contrast where there is an interesting outline in the design, the silhouette effect of the dark tracery of leaves on a white background for example. The petals of a dark flower with an unusual shape should overlap a pale neighbour – for example, place the pale curling tendrils of white bryony on a dark green background, they would be wasted on one of cream. The threefold colour contrast between a flower design and its background, then possibly a mount and lastly the frame can be very effective, but remember that flowers by the time they are dried and pressed are invariably softer in shade than when they were growing, and placing them against too great a colour contrast can overpower their gentle beauty.

Line The artistic line which runs through a graceful design may well depend upon the choice of the flower material. The natural growth of flowers on their stems and the manner in which the leaves thrust or curl must influence the design you create with them, and the way they are laid in the arrangement will ensure that their position enhances the flow of the line (see diagram 49). It is a feeling for flowers, an instinct in your eye, which confirm where the line flows in a design. There will almost inevitably be a focal point in your design, a seemingly natural place to which the line leads the eye and where you can site your largest bloom and concentrate the brightest colours.

Shape The shape of a design depends either upon the natural growing shape of the flowers and leaves you are using or upon the shape of the frame (see diagram 50). A design made from the wandering stem, leaves and flower clusters of jasmine, for example, precludes anything except a graceful, flowing shape, while the sturdy upright stance of lily-of-the-valley requires a pattern where the lines are upright and spikiness replaces flow. A round frame may demand a circular design, but a rectangular picture frame will tolerate almost any shape of design provided the size is correct. It is a question of 'eye', one's own visual taste and a sensitivity to the growing plant.

Style Flowers are obliging things, only too happy to stand side by side with others of differing shapes and hues. They will mix together in a herbaceous border, or blend gracefully even though they are planted in stiff rows, and you have only to watch the flower arranger at work to know that there are apparently limitless combinations of blossom and leaf. Pressed flowers and leaves are the same, even though their colours may be slightly muted, and you must always experiment. Remember that you are working in a two-dimensional flat material and that any effect of depth in a picture can only be achieved by careful use of colour. Bright, strong tones tend to come forward, while pale shades that repeat the background will recede. An ornate design,

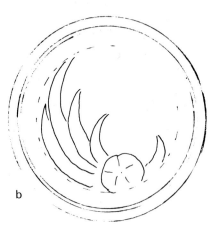

Diagram 49 Artistic lines
a. Focal point in the centre – at least six leaf tips are equidistant from edge of frame
b. Curving design repeats line of circular frame – focal point at base of arrangement
c. Focal point held by largest flower at base of design – small flowers recede into distance
d. Emphasis just below centre. A strong-coloured and largest flower placed here, while the smaller flowers below accentuate this

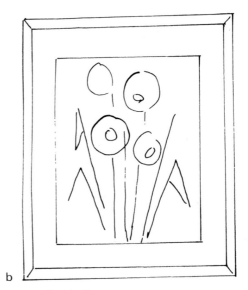

a · · · b

busy with all the flowers of the summer, can be very rewarding both to create and to look at – identifying small flowers once they are pressed and in a picture can be an amusing occupation!

Dyes Florists sometimes use artificial dyes to either deepen or change the natural colours in the flowers they sell. It is always unsatisfactory to press and use such flowers in your pictures. The chemical dye will not fade, and after a few months the petals that have been 'dipped' will look harsh and unnaturally bright amongst the others.

Diagram 50 The shape of a design
a. A bunch of flowers set in a mount
b. A natural style of arrangement within a mount, the flowers 'growing' out of the base

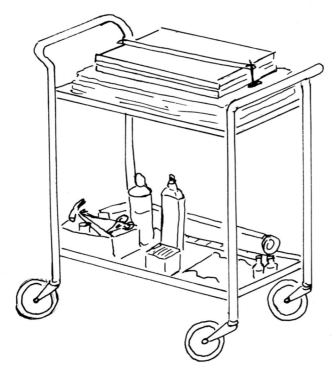
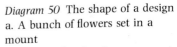

Diagram 51 Trolley with all equipment for making pictures. Upper tray holds flower press on top of layers of blotting paper which have pressed flowers ready for use inside them.
Lower tray holds boxes containing scissors, tweezers, small hammer, screw-eyes, pins etc., bottles of glass cleaner and adhesive, a roll of paper for backing, a ruler and clean soft cloths

Equipment The basic equipment for flower pressing and making pictures (see diagram 51) is cheap and simple to find, and the following list should cover all your needs. Further information on important pieces of equipment (marked with an *) can be found listed under alphabetical headings.

*adhesive
*blotting paper
biros (selection)
compass
guillotine (expensive but not
    essential)
hammer (small)
pencils (HB and 3B, good
    quality)
pliers (small – known as
    jewellers' pliers)
*press
rubber
ruler (good quality plastic or
    metal)
scissors (1 small for trimming
    flowers; 1 large for paper)
Stanley knife
staple gun (useful but not
    essential)
storage containers
tacks/gimp pins/veneer pins
travelling press
tweezers (small eyebrow
    variety)

Tools and repair materials necessary for frame alterations and repairs can be found under 'Frames'.

Fabrics Cotton, linens, silks, dupions – there is a long, long list of possible fabrics to choose from when you are deciding on a base and background for your pressed flowers. There are those made from natural fibres and those which are purely 'man-made'. It is impossible to lay down hard-and-fast rules as to the suitability of any particular material for the background of a picture, but you must take into account the size and style of the frame, and the size and colour of the flowers you want to use. You will be ill-advised to use a very coarse weave in a tiny frame, for example, and very thin 'fly-away' nylon will be very difficult to control in a huge one. A frame of bright gold may well embarrass a tweed, although the same cloth will be perfectly at home in a plain wood, modern moulding. Very shiny surfaces and those with a pile such as velvet are not easy to use. Always consider the reverse of a material as well as the right side and remember that inexpensive fabrics such as 'linings' can be excellent.

The colour range of cheap, man-made materials is often narrow, and the shades can be harsh and basic. Natural fibres take the more subtle shades better, and cottons and silks in particular can often boast a fine range of colours. Do not be put off by the high cost of some of the more exotic fabrics – remember that you will require very little length for a flower picture. Look for materials in shops that sell both dress and furnishing fabrics.

Ferns Ferns can be found in damp ditches and in woods; they love the shade of a north wall and abound in the western parts of the United Kingdom. (Diagram 52) There are small delicate ferns not more than a few inches high, while the largest varieties are more easily measured in feet! A number of freely growing indigenous ferns are too large and coarse for pressing in toto. Many of them, however, will yield up small side-fronds which will dry extremely well, retaining both their bright green colour and their deeply toothed outlines. Some of these larger ferns will have dark-coloured spots where the spores are produced on their reverse sides, and the decorative effect will survive the weeks in the press. Young fronds are often curled tightly in the spring and are very difficult to press on account of their thickness. The spiky young fronds of hard fern are the exception to this rule and will dry very well indeed. The smaller type of ferns such as the common polypody and the two commonest spleenworts produce very diminutive fronds shaped like those of a mature plant which fit easily on to the blotting paper.

Make sure that ferns are free from rain and dew before they go into the press. Always inspect the undersides for signs of ripe spores which make unusual patterns.

Winter pressing is greatly helped by the availability of ferns grown in greenhouses. Firms that specialise in indoor plants often grow and sell a useful variety of ferns all the year round. A list of these ferns which can be used in your pictures can be found at the end of the section on winter.

A list of some common ferns (length of fronds is given in cm):
black spleenwort (10cm to 45cm)
bracken or brake (grows to 180cm)
broad buckler fern (30cm to 130cm)
common polypody (10cm to 40cm)
dwarf male fern (15cm to 50cm)
hard fern (15cm to 50cm)
hard shield fern (30cm to 90cm)
hay scented buckler fern (15cm to 60cm)
maidenhair spleenwort (5cm to 35cm)
scaly male fern (40cm to 90cm)
soft shield fern (30cm to 120cm)

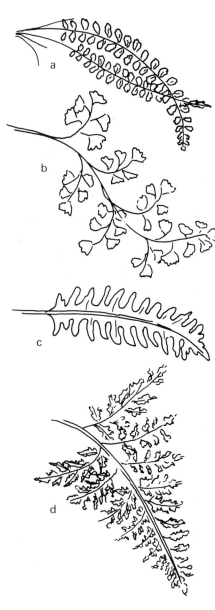

Diagram 52 Ferns
a. *Asplenium trichomanes* (Spleenwort)
b. *Adiantum capillus veneris* (Maidenhair, rare in the wild – a common house plant)
c. *Polypodium vulgare* (Common polypody)
d. *Cystoperis fragilis* (Brittle bladder fern)

Flowers – Types for pressing Essentially, when you press, you are drying out natural plant material which has a considerable amount of water in it. Once in the press the pressure exerted upon the minute cells in the plant causes them to rupture and release their moisture, which is then absorbed by the blotting paper. It follows, therefore, that on the whole the plants which are simplest and quickest to press are those which have a good structure of cellulose material and relatively little water retained in the cells. The succulents are arguably the most difficult subjects for pressing, while the 'grassy' types, such as flax, will cause no trouble. 'Fleshy' flowers such as stephanotis and lilies, which exude a lot of moisture, are also very susceptible to mould.

The shape of the flower, the perianth, too, can make for failure or success in the press. A blossom with a trumpet, a big spur or petals like a ballet dancer's skirt will be difficult to press, and may well emerge as a blob of shapeless colour. Try to imagine how the petals will fold once they are in the press. You may have to trim some of them away, or you may even discard the idea of pressing the perianth whole and take it to bits, pressing petals, pistil, stamens and sepals separately. The beautiful passion flower has to be pressed in this manner. Remember that all flowers have to be reduced to two dimensions – they will become paper-thin, delicate things when you finally take them from the press. While a common buttercup will press easily, a thistle will not. Small flowers which grow in clusters will usually have to be separated from each other before pressing.

Flowers impractical for pressing
Examples of 'fleshy' types:
African violets
bluebells
hyacinths
lilies
orchids
Examples of awkward shape:
buddleias
daffodils
dianthus of all kinds
lilac
poppies – large
roses – large
thistles

Frames Inexpensive frames can be bought ready-made from shops or they can be made up to your own requirements by a framer. The choice of style will probably be rather limited in the first instance, but if you decide on the second approach you may well be bewildered by the wide choice of mouldings offered to you. Always go to a good framer and seek his advice, his experienced eye should assist you. He will make the frame and quote you a price which may or may not include glass and backing. (If you intend to use the 'free' method in

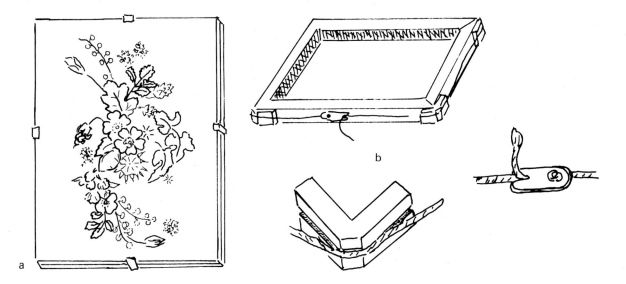

making your picture then you will require hardboard backing, but if you follow the 'fixed' method you may find a stiff cardboard backing just as satisfactory.)

Round and oval frames are factory-made and many of them these days are imported. It will pay you to 'shop around', for there is a wide divergence in both price and quality. Make sure that 'gold' really is 'gold leaf' and that the wood is not a plastic composition.

'Klipframe' These modern frames (diagram 53a) are composed of a base of strong card or hardboard and a matching piece of glass with metal spring clips spaced around the edges to hold the two surfaces together. Pressed flowers can be laid on the board and held safely in position once the clips are fixed. 'Klipframes' are made in several sizes. A small one about 6in square will cost about £2.00.

It is not difficult to make your own light-weight frames. Moulding can be bought from frame shops and you can usually arrange for the lengths to be cut and mitred for you. Pin and glue the four corners – small clamps or even a tight circle of string will hold the ends in place while the glue dries. (You can buy an inexpensive set of four plastic 'corners' and a running noose of cord from D.I.Y. shops (diagram 53b).) Use a strong glue and small veneer pins for the corners.

The cost of frames is considerable these days so take care in your choice of moulding as a mistake will be expensive. If you can order a large number of similar frames at one time the factory principle of mass production will hold good and you can expect a reduction in price.

When choosing a frame for your pressed flowers (diagram 54) remember that they are relatively soft and gentle in effect and they can easily be overpowered by too heavy or too bright a frame. An old frame therefore can often be a most suitable surround for your picture

Diagram 53
a. Pictures without frames (spring clips hold glass to board)
b. Stanley frame clamp showing detail of assembly

Figure 15 A 'Klipframe' flower picture. This arrangement of leaves, buds and a single flower of hellebore has been given greater depth by this type of frame. The thin layer of perspex held by simple clips to the plain card back gives a slight shadow to the pressed material. The wide variation in tone between the different leaves makes it most pleasing to the eye. There are ferns and Virginia creeper, silverweed and ivy and a single bending stem of cow-parsley

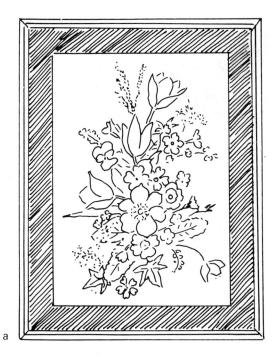

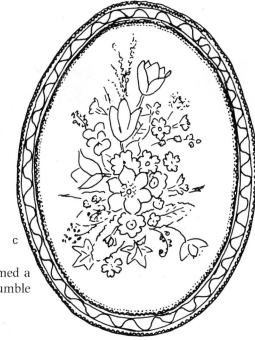

Diagram 54 The effect of three
different frames on the same
arrangement of spring flowers
a. Simple modern frame with a
mount
b. Small modern frame of narrow
moulding
c. Oval frame

– the gold will be mellowed by age, or the shiny varnish dimmed a
little. Look in secondhand shops and salerooms and visit the jumble
sales.

Framing up Have ready the following equipment:

small pair of pliers (jeweller's pliers are excellent)
small tacks or veneer pins
light 'tack' hammer
roll of sticky tape or paper
paper to cover back of frame (coloured 'art' or 'sugar' paper or
wallpaper)
scissors
small labels, pens.

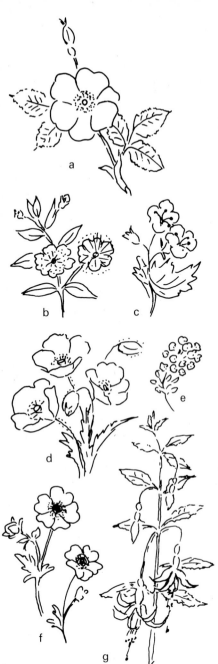

Cover your working surface with a thick soft cloth and clean both frame and glass thoroughly.

BE ESPECIALLY CAREFUL AT THIS POINT WHEN DOING A 'FREE METHOD' PICTURE.

Place the cleaned glass gently on top of the flowers, place the frame over the glass, pinch very tightly together and turn over and lay the assembly face downwards on the table. Take a sharp-ended tack and hold it in the pliers. Push down the side of the picture firmly into the frame where you are going to nail and press the tack point into the wood of the frame just above the point where the picture back lies in the rebate. Give three or four smart taps with the hammer to drive in the tack until it is firm. It should be driven in at a slight angle and subsequently bent over gently till the tack head rests against the picture back. Make sure that the picture is pressed into the frame equally and hammer tacks in all the way round. When using the 'fixed' method (see 'Methods') you may have to place some sort of extra backing behind the flower picture. Newspaper, cotton blanket material or magazines can provide this extra padding, but the top layer must be firm and fairly rigid – stiff card or thin hardboard is satisfactory. Use your picture glass as a template when cutting the pieces of backing. When following the 'free' method, extra backing will only be necessary if the frame is a deep one.

Instructions

1 First place the frame with clean glass and flower picture in place, face downwards on table.

2 Cut pieces of newspaper or similar padding to size and place in frame.

3 Cut stiff card or hardboard to size and place on top.

4 Use small tacks, nails or staples to fasten picture in place, using a small hammer or a staple gun.

5 Cover nail ends with strips of paper or masking tape.

6 Cut to size and stick down paper to give a tidy finish and to keep out dust.

Garden Flowers It would be nice indeed to be able to press every single flower that grows in a well-stocked English garden, but sadly this will never be possible. There are too many large and beautiful blooms which must defeat all efforts to press them. Double poppies and tall delphiniums, great blowsy roses and Canterbury bells, antirrhinums and showy asters – there is a long list of much-loved flowers that must be left to bloom undisturbed or else picked only to decorate the house in a vase.

If you are a keen gardener, however, you can grow your own flowers for pressing in the garden, giving yourself a double pleasure. You will know how many flowers to reserve for your pressing requirements and you will be able to pick the exact size of bloom that you require.

Diagram 55 Garden flowers for pressing
a. rose
b. myrtle
c. phaecelia
d. poppy
e. sweet alyssum
f. potentilla
g. fuchsia

Many of the general guide lines on deciding which flowers to pick for pressing are identical with those governing wild flowers, but in the garden there is also the unexpected factor of size. One of the best known aims of a gardener is to have a good rich soil and to grow very large and lush blooms. This often results, so far as the flower presser is concerned, in having a great number of blooms that are far too large for the press. When you are searching the gardens for flowers to press, you will quickly find that the second best or even the third best blooms are the ones for your needs. Look on the shady side of the plant, or wait for the second flowering.

The best-shaped flowers for full-face pressing are those with open faces, the daisy or rose types. Star-shaped flowers like allium florets are also very easy candidates. Snowdrops, lily-of-the-valley, bleeding heart and many others prefer to be pressed in profile. Many flowers with tubular corollas or with 'winged' or 'spurred' arrangements of petals are very awkward to press successfully – the foxglove and larkspur are two obvious members of this category. Flowers, too, that are circular or 'pom-pom' in shape are also unrewarding. We have put lists of garden flowers which we recommend for pressing at the end of each of the four seasonal chapters. (Some flowers continue to bloom through the following season, and these have been noted.)

Glass Take your frame to any glass-cutter and he will probably cut the glass for you on the spot. You will need the weight known as 'picture' glass, 2mm thick and sold by the square foot. The minimum quantity normally charged for is one square foot, though if you present him with a very small frame a friendly glass-cutter may well use up an oddment of glass just to oblige you. It is possible to get non-reflective glass, or diffused reflection as it is correctly called, but there is little point in paying the considerable extra cost because flower pictures should hang away from the light and the problem of a strong reflection should not occur. You may be fortunate enough to acquire very old frames. These sometimes have the original thin glass in them; it may be very thin and even have tiny bubbles and swirls in it. Be careful not to crack it when you are framing your picture, it will repay the extra care and give a soft clarity to the flowers. It used to be said in the trade before the First World War that some glass was so thin it could be cut with a pair of scissors if held under water! So beware its fragility. Convex glass is also used to cover flower designs, but it is expensive.

Gold Gold colour on frames can either be real gold leaf or imitation, inexpensive gold paint. Gold leaf will be bright with a good shine and old age will only mellow, not spoil, its beauty. Gold paint, however, although it starts bright, may discolour and grow dull after relatively few years and an application of a good 'gold' wax polish such as 'Treasure Gold Wax' will improve its appearance greatly. Small repairs to gold frames are fairly simple, but it must be appreciated that, because it is very difficult to match gold shades, large repaired areas may never blend in satisfactorily. Your frame stands in danger of becoming 'piebald' at the end of an extensive repair job! For small repairs to gold frames we would recommend the use of liquid gold paint such as 'Liquid Leaf' – choose the closest matching shade and correct any further dissimilarity with the cautious addition of artist's paints, such as Raw Umber or Vandyke Brown. Cheap 'Gold Spray' can be used to cheerful effect on Christmas cards.

Grasses Most of the Graminae family – known as grasses to most people – press very well. Nearly all of them are dry, pithy plants and it is usually only great size which will prevent you from placing them easily between the blotting paper pages. A few grasses such as barley or cat's tails have very thick heads and although they will dry satisfactorily they are awkward to use in arrangements. Remember that unless you are seeking a special fluffy effect, grasses for pressing should be picked as soon as they come out. The dry seeds tend to fall.

Hardboard This useful builder's material is excellent as a base for your flowers, when you are following the 'free' method, or as a straightforward backing for your picture frame. It can be bought from hardware stores. The commonest stocked size is known as 'door skin', 6ft 6in × 2ft 6in, which is probably far larger than you will need. Ask the shop to order a smaller sheet, 4ft × 2ft, and specify the thickness, $\frac{1}{8}$in. (Some shopkeepers may be able to cut you a small piece to your exact requirements.) When you cut your own hardboard use a general-purpose saw with fine teeth and sandpaper the edges smooth – it is a good thing to round off the corners very slightly if you are making a base board which is to be padded. When cutting hardboard for your frame remember to allow extra size for the depth of the rebate – if the glass has already been cut, it will make a template for you. Small sheets of hardboard cut to the same size as your blotting paper are useful for interleaving in your press.

Heat-sealing This is a relatively new technique used in the covering of fragile or delicate surfaces with a permanent plastic skin to protect them. It can be used successfully to cover pressed flowers mounted on paper or card, and even when they are fixed on to material, provided that the surface is smooth. With the correct application of heat and pressure to a thin film of plastic placed over the 'picture', there will be a sufficient 'bonding' between the two surfaces for permanent adhesion. This covering can also be used to seal and protect a small flower design fixed into a mount. If it is done well the entire surface will be protected and the coating will be almost invisible.

The 'heat treatment' technique requires special equipment and expertise in using it, and you should enquire at your local picture framing shop to see if you can get it done there. The final result is surprisingly good, and it is a far cry from the crinkles and the shine of most D.I.Y. plastic coatings. (The wall calendar featured on the back jacket has been sealed with this method.) Always ask for an estimate before you have any work done.

Ink Black and coloured inks, including gold and silver, are often needed for decorative purposes when you are making flower cards. Flower designs can be enhanced by a single or double inked border, greetings can be written in the same colour and your creation can be initialled or autographed. Flower pictures can also be made more interesting for the botanist by an attractively written label on the back of the frame, noting where the flowers came from and their names – whether you write 'sneezewort' or *Achillea ptarmica* is up to you! Watermans have a fine range of colours in their inks and these can be found in most good art shops. You will need a pen holder and draughtsman's nibs.

Metallic inks such as gold and silver require frequent and vigorous shaking of the bottle when using them – practise on a spare bit of paper until you get the knack of making the ink flow steadily from the nib.

Ironing Flowers Occasionally flowers will press unevenly and one or two petals will be crumpled. Using tweezers, lay the whole flower between two pieces of clean blotting paper and, with the tip of a very cool iron, smooth it over. Some flowers will even stand a direct ironing, but experiment first with an expendable failure. Leaves too, can be ironed successfully, and this will help to shorten the drying time.

Iron-on Lining This is ironed on to the reverse of fabrics and is very useful for giving weight and substance, especially to any fine material destined to have pressed flowers stuck down on to it. Use it for making Bible markers, pulpit and lectern falls in particular, and also for flower pictures where the 'fixed' method is employed. Iron-on lining can be bought from most large stores and from material shops and haberdasheries. Often known as 'Vilene', it is available in both black and white and is made in various weights ranging from the very fine, for use with silks and thin cottons, to the much heavier qualities. All types of 'iron-on' lining are matt on one side and slightly glazed on the other; the shiny side is where the adhesive is. Place the fabric that requires backing on a clean ironing board and ensure that it is free of creases. Cut the lining exactly to size and place it 'shiny' side down on the fabric. Press with a medium/cool iron without heavy pressure. The heat will melt the impregnated surface of the lining and the two surfaces will stick together. Be careful not to leave any air bubbles in between the fabrics, an overall bonding is best.

Leaves Pressing leaves for use in your pictures and cards is almost as important as pressing flowers, and in fact it is perfectly possible to create charming designs using them alone. Leaves will be judged by their size, shape, colour and surface texture, and the lists of seasonal garden plants, wild flowers, trees, shrubs and creepers will help you to choose which to put in the press. Remember that some leaves change colour in the autumn. Some, too, will alter in shade in the press. Always look for leaves that have distinctive colour and shape, because ultimately when you are creating a design with them these are the factors which will be most useful to you. You will need to include in your pressed material the strong red of acer and late-picked blackberry leaves, along with the silver-grey of willow and artemisia and the differing greens of lily-of-the-valley and the common nettle. The shape of leaves too can vary enormously, as our drawings and picture designs show. Try to include as many differing shapes as you can – unless a single coloured leaf has a sharp, interesting or delicate outline it may easily be visually dull.

Diagram 56 Distinctive leaves
a. clematis
b. sumach
c. Virginia creeper
d. acer
e. A design of 'silver' leaves
   showing the different shapes.
   Dark buds of elder match the
   rich brown of the mount

90

The factors which predetermine whether or not a leaf will press successfully are often similar to those that govern the pressing of flowers, and it is simpler to draw attention to those characteristics which may cause failure than to attempt to list every quality which will survive any amount of pressing.

Fleshy leaves, such as gloxinia and African violets, will not press.

Rounded needles like those of Scots pine, and even the tiny ones on heather, tend to dry and shrivel.

Hairy leaves like those of *Stachys lanata* are difficult.

Curly-edged leaves – from those of the slightly curly garden primula to the much convoluted fern *Nephrolepsis exaltata* – all press badly.

Old and damaged leaves are never worth pressing.

In hot weather very young and delicate leaves must go direct from plant to press.

Thick leaves, particularly those with shiny surfaces, take a long time to dry.

Discard any leaves with insect eggs on them – small creatures have a bad habit of hatching out in the warm safety of your press and of eating the specimens!

Dry, pithy leaves such as bamboo and small house palms tend to fade badly.

Leaves with heavily indented surfaces, such as those of some 'foliage' plants, members of the cactus family and all the true succulents, are reluctant candidates for your press.

Always experiment with pressing new types of leaves, but the following notes reminding you of varieties that are easy and rewarding to prepare will help to keep your store full:

A few plants have leaves that are one colour on the top and another on the underside. Mugwort must be one of the most common examples of this type; it is dark green above and silvery grey beneath. Wild raspberry has leaves with the same attractive bi-coloured pattern.

Grey leaves from what is often know as silver foliage plants (diagram 56e) are always assured of a place in your designs; senecio, salvia, artemisia – there is a long list.

Wild flowers, too, frequently have little leaves which at first sight take second place to the flowers but which will dry and press beautifully. Herb Robert, wild strawberry and yellow cinquefoil are three well-known plants in this category.

Autumn foliage is one of the best sources of bright colour for your pictures.

Always pick leaves immediately they colour completely – left on the tree too long they will usually shrivel and fade in the press.

Leaves from greenhouse-grown 'foliage' plants and ferns are invaluable for winter pressing and there is advice about pressing them in the Winter section with lists of recommended varieties.

Diagram 57 The free method of
mounting flowers
a. Place hardboard on wadding,
mark outline with felt-tip pen and
cut out
b. Place hardboard on fabric (do
not mark with pen), cut out
allowing 4cm (1½in) extra all
round. Check grain of fabric
c. Place wadding on rough side of
hardboard and cover with fabric,
right side up
d. Turn over and cut off corners
of fabric. Run thin line of
adhesive around edge of
hardboard and stick fabric down
all round. Check grain
e. For circular and oval frames

Lichen Grey lichen can be found in abundance in the western
districts of the United Kingdom. It grows on trees, and on the sides of
old buildings, banks and walls facing the prevailing rains, and it
especially favours dead trees. The long feathery trails can be pressed
and used to good effect in flower pictures, as can the fan-shaped silver
variety which usually grows tucked into the crevices of old walls. Try
to dry all excess moisture from lichens before you put them into the
press.

Methods for Making Flower Pictures
(Free method and fixed method)

Free Method This is where the flowers and leaves are laid loose upon a
padded background; only when they are arranged to your complete
satisfaction, achieving the artistic effect you desire, is the glass laid on
top of them to hold them in place. The frame is then placed on top, the
picture turned face down on the table, and small tacks or nails driven

into the sides of the frame, thus holding the picture in. The pressure exerted between the glass and the padded background is very considerable and the flowers will be held tightly in place.

The first step is to prepare the base or background. It is essential to use thin wadding underneath all fabric to give a padded effect and to prevent the flowers from slipping out of place. For a padded fabric background, first cut a base of thin hardboard to the internal rebate measurements of the frame. Smooth the edge and corners with sandpaper. Cut your fabric at least 4cm (1½in) larger than the hardboard and iron it free of creases. Cut a piece of thin wadding exactly the same size as the hardboard, iron out creases, place it on the hardboard smooth side down and trim. Lay the fabric, right side down, in the centre of it and line it up with the grain of the cloth. Place the hardboard exactly on top of the wadding, rough side down. Run a thin line of adhesive 2cm (½in) from the edge all round the edges of the hardboard. Starting with the top, and then going to the bottom of the base, fold the fabric over the edges of the hardboard and stick it down onto the smooth back. Check constantly that the grain runs true and pull the fabric *taut* across the wadding. Fold the fabric neatly at the corners and glue also. Allow the adhesive to dry and the background will be ready for use (diagram 57).

For a card or paper background first cut your piece of hardboard in the same manner as explained above and then, using it as a template, cut out your chosen paper or card. (If you wish to stick it on to the hardboard, use a mild paper adhesive such as 'Pritt Stick'. Stronger glues can leave a series of shrink marks.)

Now the background is ready for your flowers. Select from your store of pressed materials the leaves, buds and blossoms that will suit the frame and the background for both colour and size. All pressed material must be handled with tweezers only. Think of your design as a shape on the material and start with the topmost point. Select a leaf and place it on the background. Then decide how low in the frame the design will go down to, take another leaf or piece of stalk and put that in position too. Mark out the furthest extent of the design shape on either side and then proceed to build inwards. Move the flowers and leaves carefully so that they not only fill in the design towards the focal point, but also complement each other as neighbours. Flowers can either blend with each other or contrast, but they should not clash or be of identical shade. When completed, place the glass on top of flowers to hold them in place. (Always ensure that the glass is clean.) For further instructions see 'Framing up'.

Most designs have a focal point, a loosely determined spot where the lines of the design meet and to which the eye is led. It will hold your finest flower and must subtly dominate, either by colour or size, the whole picture. A flower picture without this central focal point can easily resemble wallpaper.

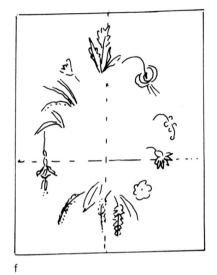

f

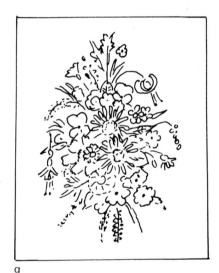

g

slash fabric all round and pull taut gently and with care
f. Making the outline
g. Filling in the design with flowers

Fixed Method As the name suggests, here the flowers and leaves are stuck down on to the background with an adhesive. Although it is perfectly possible to use the padded base as a prepared background for a picture, it is equally simple to fix the flowers on to a piece of fabric (preferably lined with an 'iron-on' lining to give it extra body), and to dispense with the wadding. First cut a piece of fabric a little bigger than the whole frame and back it evenly with iron-on lining. This will give the fabric more body and make it easier to work on (see p. 89). This now is your background for the picture. Take another similar sized and coloured piece of fabric or paper to work on initially with your flowers; this is your temporary background. Place the frame on it, have your flowers to hand and you are ready to begin. Work within the empty frame and build up a design in exactly the same way as for the 'free' method. When it is completed to your satisfaction then you are ready to start fixing everything down with an adhesive. You have got to transfer the flowers, one by one, from the temporary background to the prepared background, and it is obvious that in order to do this you must set aside the entire centre of the design in order to reach the flowers and leaves which make up the basic outline. If you experience difficulty in remembering the exact position of each flower once it is moved, then it may help if you take a tracing of the design as it lies loose on the temporary background and use this to help you to re-form your design exactly as you stick.

First remove the frame and place a clean sheet of glass over the flowers. Take a square of tracing paper and lay it carefully on top, and draw round the outline with a soft 3B pencil. Mark in the position of the key flowers – especially their centres. Lay the prepared background on a very thick folded blanket and, having lifted the tracing paper from the flowers, place it on the background, making sure that the design lies correctly in relation to the grain of the material (place the frame over the drawing to test this). Pin the tracing down firmly at the corners or clips (diagram 58). Have ready a supply of clean, sharp, ordinary dressmaker's pins. Take one and push it through the paper into the background and the blanket at the topmost point of the flower design. Push it in at an angle, pointing inwards so that the pinhead is eventually lying against the paper and just *inside* the pencil line. Continue to 'pin' the tracing on to the background, following the picture, until you have the whole of the outline fixed at the main points by pins. This should include the centres of most of the flowers. Ensure that all pins are pushed fully down into the background and the underlying blanket. Carefully lift the paper away from the pins, allowing the pinheads to tear through the thin tracing paper. Use these pins as markers for placing the flowers and leaves. It is also possible to make your picture using the traced copy as a pattern and to dispense with the pins altogether.

Work always within the frame. Have ready a small amount of 'Copydex' or similar adhesive in a small flat dish, and a small sharpened stick (a matchstick will do very well). Lift the flowers which

a

b

form the centre of the design with tweezers and put them to one side. Take up the topmost leaf in your tweezers and smear a little adhesive on the top and the bottom on the reverse side. Place it in position on the background, using the top pin as a marker. Repeat this procedure with the rest of the pressed material, transferring the outline of the design first. Work inwards and stick everything down firmly but with the minimum of adhesive. Keep the design shape well in mind as you re-form it, and remove the pins once they have served their purpose as markers. Remember to keep the flowers pointing the correct way in the design – most flower faces require to be the right, that is the natural, way up. Build in towards the focal point, which should be the last main flower that you stick down. Add small trims, tiny buds, tendrils (and stalks if you are using them) last of all.

When the design is complete use the glass as a template and cut the material to fit into the frame. Make sure the flower design is exactly central and that the threads in the cloth are parallel to the frame edge. Make sure that the pins are all clean – an elderly, unused pin can make a horrible mark. It is not recommended that any marks should be made on a background with pencil, dye, carbon, etc. since they will have to be covered up by flowers, and this precludes any slight change in the position of the pressed material that you may wish to make. Be sparing with the pins; even pinholes can mark a finely woven material.

Extreme care must be taken not to spill any adhesive on to the background material – it will almost certainly leave a shiny mark and spoil the picture.

Diagram 58 Creating the design
a. Flowers laid loose on card background
b. Tracing paper laid over design held in place by clips. Main features of flowers outlined in pencil

95

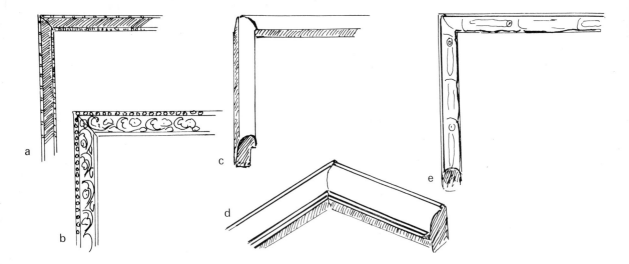

Diagram 59 Moulding for frames
a. Hogarth
b. Heavy gesso and gilt
c. Plain gold 'Hockey stick'
d. Modern gold
e. Gilt bamboo

Tracing paper is best bought in flat packs (not in the usual rolls) from stationers.
For framing of flower designs made by both methods see p. 85, 'Frames'.

Mould This is a serious thing which flower pressers must guard against. It is most prevalent during a wet summer, when the minute spores may already be present on the flowers and leaves when you pick them, although invisible to the natural eye. Left alone in a pleasantly warm press they will multiply at a frightening speed. Mould appears as black and grey marks on both flowers and blotting paper and will spread and infect everything across a page of blotting paper if left undisturbed. To guard against it, ensure that all flowers and leaves are dry when put into the press, and during a particularly wet summer check them regularly. Keep your presses tightly screwed down, and if you find any mould forming discard and burn both flowers and blotting paper.

Mouldings This is the name given by framemakers to the long strips of shaped, embossed and surface-coloured wood which they cut and fashion into frames (diagram 59). A good framemaker will carry a wide range of mouldings and samples of many more which you can order through him. He will probably stock both English and foreign mouldings. The price of moulding is worked out on the length, and although metrication has arrived in theory you may still be offered 'so much per foot'. The price per unit length is determined by the width, the simplicity of shape, the quantity of ornamentation, surface, colour and popularity. Some mouldings are easily scratched; for example, those covered with real gold leaf are extremely delicate, and it is essential to treat these with care and to lay them on a soft surface when you are working on them. Good quality moulding is always

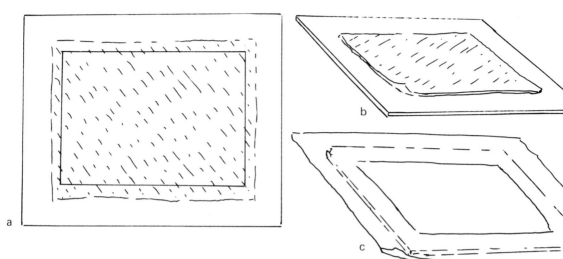

made of wood and it should not be so hard that it is virtually impossible to knock the tacks in. Cheap plastic frames and mouldings are seldom a good investment. Moulding for round and oval frames is fashioned professionally and is only sold as completed frames.

Mounting Flowers When some flowers emerge from the press their petals will appear to be almost transparent. They may still retain their own colour when lying on the white blotting paper, but as soon as they are lifted from it and placed in a flower arrangement you will find that the colour of their new background will shine through. These flowers must be mounted or backed before they can be used. There are two ways of doing this. The best way is to place one flower on top of another of similar size and shape in order to get the required degree of opacity. This can be awkward as flowers are seldom exactly the same size and it is also wasteful of flower material. Alternatively, back the flower with a small piece of thin paper; tissue paper of the same colour is the best but any thin white paper will suffice. Be discriminating in backing your flowers – they can look stiff and artificial.

Instructions
Cut a circle of paper a little larger than the flower.
Place a speck of 'Copydex' or similar adhesive in the centre of it and stick the flower down on to it.
Leave to dry.
With a small and sharp pair of scissors cut round the paper 'petals', being extremely careful not to 'nick' the real petals while you are doing it.

Mounts Mounts are made from thick card and are used within a frame to surround and set off the picture. The colour range in mounting card is very wide, the surface finish usually matt and although it is possible to make one's own, to cut by eye a faultless

Diagram 60 Making a padded background for use with a mount
a. Cut hardboard to fit inside of frame. Lay hardboard smooth side up on table. Cut wadding 3cm ($1\frac{1}{8}$in) larger all round than aperture of rectangular mount
b. Place wadding on hardboard. (A small spot of adhesive will keep it in place.)
c. Lay fabric over board and wadding and cut it 3cm ($1\frac{1}{8}$in) larger all round than the hardboard. Check grain of fabric with the edges of the hardboard. Turn over, put line of adhesive 2.5cm (1in) in from the edges and stick down fabric. Mount can be laid in place while flowers are arranged
d. Frame complete with the padding ready inside mount. Glass will be added when design is complete

mount with bevelled edge is very difficult indeed to achieve. It is usually best to buy them from picture framers or art shops, they are not very expensive and the expert can cut one quickly. Mounts can be edged around the aperture with a series of fine inked lines and this can add a great deal of delicacy to a large flower picture. When using a mount it is easiest to follow the 'fixed' method of making flower pictures, but success is possible if you want to leave your flowers 'free', providing you use terylene wadding on your base as this has extra 'bounce' (diagram 60).

Nibs Drawing-nibs of different sizes can be bought from art and craft shops. The width of the nib point will govern the breadth of line. Some nibs are cut straight across the point and these will be excellent for ruling border lines. For lettering and ornamentation the angled pointed nibs can be easier to use. Nibs are made with or without a reservoir; this, as the name suggest, is a very small flap device on the nib which automatically holds extra ink until it is needed. When using 'gold' ink the best nib to use is the long old-fashioned variety; any flat, slow-flowing nib will quickly clog, the powdered metal being retained at the top of the nib and only the clear liquid flowing on to the paper. Nibs vary in cost from a few pence to much more for a very broad, reservoir nib. Practise the technique on scrap paper before embarking on drawing fine lines and ornamentation on a flower card.

Paper There is such a wide range of papers on the market suitable for backgrounds in pressed flower pictures, that it can be difficult to choose between them. You will have to consider colour, of course, but the type of surface is also important. This can range from the high gloss to the rough, broken-textured type, and it is a matter of personal preference which you choose.

Paper is usually sold in sheets and these may vary in size. There is no standard measurement, and imported papers are invariably different in size from their English counterparts. Price certainly comes into the choice, because you will have to buy a complete sheet of paper even though you may only require a piece less than six inches square.

Try to choose a paper which you will be happy to use again and again. Always consider inexpensive papers; a matt or even a slightly broken surface is not necessarily unattractive with pressed flowers. The main weakness of cheap papers is that they often tear easily, and need careful handling. Papers can be bought at art and craft shops and at good stationers, and in London there is an excellent shop which specialises in paper and nothing else. Always roll paper when storing it, and use a guillotine for cutting it if you can. Stationers and art shops will stock the types of paper that you need.

Plastic Coverings Various plastic coverings can be bought at stationers and D.I.Y. shops. There is also a mail order firm which can supply these coverings (see List of Suppliers). They can be used very successfully for covering pressed flower designs in order to protect them. 'Non-reflective' and 'shiny' types are equally satisfactory.

Presses A flower press can either be home-made or bought from a shop. The only criterion is that it shall exert a hard and uniform pressure on the flowers and leaves inside. The basic flower press has two rigid sheets of wood between which there is room for layers of blotting paper, and the whole can be pinched together by large screws and butterfly nuts. These screws can either thread through four corner holes in both top and bottom or can hold together metal bands which encircle the entire press. It is perfectly possible to press flowers well in a variety of other and simpler ways, such as by placing them between the pages of telephone directories or in newspaper under the carpet, but we contend that a well-pressed flower is a hard-pressed one, and that you will have fewer failures if you use the screw type of press.

Homemade Press Type 1 The simplest way to make a flower press is to get two pieces of thin wood (1.5cm [$\frac{1}{2}$in] chip board is ideal). Mark and drill a hole in each of the four corners at least one inch in from the edges, making the holes large enough to accom-

Diagram 61 Home-made heavy flower press made from two pieces of chip board 30cm × 45cm × 3cm (12in × 18in × 1$\frac{1}{8}$in) crossed with iron bands 2$\frac{1}{2}$cm × 50cm × 4mm (1in × 20in × $\frac{1}{8}$in). Both top and bottom boards have a band screwed into the chip board with 4 screws placed at equal intervals. Holes are drilled 13mm ($\frac{1}{2}$in) from the band ends to take large coach bolts. Wing nuts are used to tighten the bands together

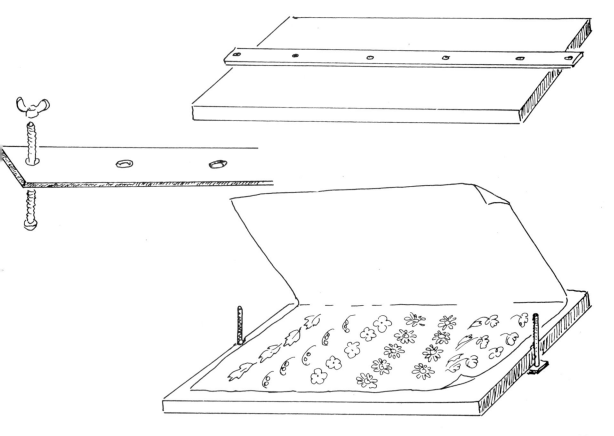

modate four long screws. (You will need four stout screws and butterfly nuts.) These rectangles of wood will be the outsides of your press and you must cut sheets of blotting paper and interleaves of card or newspaper to fit. (Remember to cut across the corners to allow for the screws.)

The success of the press will depend upon the rigidity of the outside boards in relation to the amount of blotting paper and pressed flowers you put in it. The disadvantage of using more solid pieces of wood is weight – a full press can be surprisingly heavy. Always keep your press screwed down as tightly as possible.

Homemade Press Type 2 Metal strips with holes at each end to receive the two heavy-duty screws will give extra strength and rigidity to your basic wood boards (diagram 61). These metal strips can be obtained from a hardware shop. They will need to be 5cm (2in) longer overall than the boards and must have holes drilled in the ends for the bolts or screws. (It will also be an advantage to have two small holes drilled about 10cm [4in] in from the ends to accommodate small screws to attach the bands to the boards.)

Homemade Press Type 3 The old fashioned man's trouser press is excellent; these can still be found in attics and 'jumble' sales – use hardboard interleaves.

Small travelling presses can either be bought or made at home (diagram 62). The main requirement is that they should be small and light. It is possible to buy very small flower presses about 15cm (6in) square, or once again the jumble sale may produce an old tie press which will solve your travelling problems.

A temporary 'picking' press can be made from two small squares of thin hardboard and a powerful elastic band. The band is put on over the opposing corners and will hold the flowers in place between the small squares of blotting paper until you get home to your big press. (This type of press is invaluable on a hot summer's day – just put it in your pocket before you start out!)

Diagram 62 Small lightweight flower press (obtainable in various sizes from 10cm (4in) square upwards

Pressing We recommend that you press your flowers between blotting paper. It is excellent in every way, highly absorbent and matt surfaced; also it is inexpensive and can be used over and over again. Use newspaper to interleave the blotting paper every so often throughout the press. Always put flowers and leaves of the same thickness on to the same page of blotting paper; you can place a greater number of specimens of thin, rather fragile flowers on one page than you can if they are thick and bulky flowers. Buds, in particular, make bumps in between the sheets of paper, and too many of these bumps on one page of paper can be conducive to mould forming. They may also make some petals elude the full pressure which is essential to success. Very thick flowers may take kindly to the extra thickness of a blotting paper collar (see 'Collars'). Bisect the buds with a razor and press both halves. Don't let flowers and leaves overlap in the press, each specimen needs its own clear space on the paper. Press flowers in profile as well as full face. Remember to use buds, leaves, tendrils, seed-heads, grasses and stalks, and arrange them on the sheets with material of similar thickness. Always screw the press down as tightly as you can. Leave the flowers undisturbed for a week or so (tighten the screws a little more every day), then cautiously open the press, inspect the pages, discard any specimens that show sign of mould and correct any that have wrongly folded petals. Move any particularly thick or fleshy specimens on to a dry area of paper. Screw down the press again and return it to a warm place to finish drying out.

Drying and pressing should be completed in two to eight weeks, depending on the thickness of the specimens. When the flowers are properly dry they will be very light and brittle. Take great care when you lift them from the press – they may stick slightly; always use tweezers.

Protected Varieties Rare flowers are protected in many countries of the world, and it is sensible to enquire about them before a foreign holiday if you intend to pick and press. We would encourage you always to think before you pick – one less flower growing means less seed for next year. If you find an unusual, single flower, restrain your hand; there is no particular merit in pressing a rare variety for use in a flower picture. It may not press well, and it is likely that a similarly coloured and far more common flower will do just as well. Enquire at your local public library for details of flowers protected by *The Conservation of Wild Creatures and Wild Plants Act, 1975* and by *The Wildlife and Countryside Act, 1981*.

Repairing Flowers Petals can sometimes get damaged during pressing, but a small repair with a perfect replacement petal from another flower will enable you to use it. Cut a small circle of thin white paper, a little smaller than the flower. Place a small dab of adhesive in the centre of it and lay the damaged bloom on to it. Select a 'spare' petal and very carefully slide it under the flattened stamens, so that the end is caught in the adhesive and the petal lies neatly in a proper line with its fellows. More major repairs can be carried out satisfactorily in this manner, using a paper circle as a base; you must mount all the petals separately, just touching their points, and then stick down the boss of stamens.

Repairing Frames Minor repairs such as scratching and chipping of wood or plaster can be dealt with as follows:

1 Dislodge any loose pieces from the area to be repaired. Brush free from dust.

2 Fill broken area with plastic wood or 'plastic padding', depending on the type of frame, and smooth surface to correct level. (The filler will shrink a little on drying, so leave the repair level fractionally proud of the surrounding surface.)

3 Leave to dry according to the instructions on the packet.

4 Rub down gently to the exact level of the frame with flour paper (finest sandpaper).

5 Colour to match frame. (Wood frames can be coloured with the correct shade of stain or even with a judicious application of boot polish!)

Gold frames should be repaired with plastic padding (elastic type) and rubbed smooth. Use good quality gold paint and match carefully for shade variation.

Gold-leaf frames needing repair are very difficult. A very small area can be camouflaged with gold-paint – true gold leaf will be too bright unless the frame is a new one. If there are large areas requiring repair, you will do better to regild the entire frame.

Rushes (and Sedges) Rushes belong to the juncaceae family and, like their cousins the sedges and grasses, there are quite a number of them growing in the British Isles. The flowers are usually dark brown or almost purple-black, occasionally deep green; they often appear jutting out at a sharp angle from the main stem, or sometimes at the top of the stem.

Rushes tend to grow where it is damp and will be found along ditches, beside ponds and rivers and in wet moorland. Even the salt of coastal marshes does not deter them.

Press the dark flowers when they have unfolded properly but before they become 'overblown'.

Seeds and Seed-heads Always look carefully at the seed-heads of plants; a surprising number of them will press well and provide unusual shapes for your designs (diagram 63). Most of the umbelliferae produce seed-heads which dry darker and are very useful – press the little seed-heads both separately and in their natural clusters. Willowherb and herb Robert both produce seed-heads of

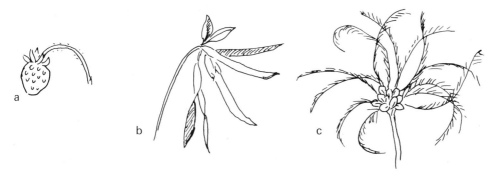

unusual shape – catch them just as they are at the point of spilling their seeds. Grasses and sorrels, ivy and clematis, grape hyacinth and even tiny strawberries will all be well worth pressing. Very large heads such as acanthus and poppy will require bisecting with a razor blade, following the same instructions as for thick buds.

Skeletonising Boil material to be skeletonised in strong detergent (3 tbls in 20 fl.oz.). Strain into sieve and rinse with cold water. Float them in a saucer and extract one by one with a finger tip. Brush away soft tissue with a small brush, leaving the exposed 'skeleton'. Dry on blotting paper.

Storing Bright sunlight and dust are destroyers of delicate pressed flowers. Once the flowers are pressed properly and completely dry take them from the press and lay them in a blotting paper folder or in a shallow cardboard box. Store these in a dry place where they are free from dust. The small cabinets such as are used by dentists are excellent for storing your flowers, but they are hard to find. Remember that flowers and leaves over an inch and a half in width must be kept flat between paper, otherwise they will curl up.

Table-mats Table-mats can be made and decorated attractively with pressed flowers. The following instructions (diagram 64) are given for making a single place-mat 20cm (8in) in diameter. (Rectangular mats can also be made but binding and finishing off corners can cause problems.)

8in diameter circle of picture glass or perspex
Similar sized flower base of felt
Similar sized mat base of hardboard or cork
Adhesive (clear drying such as 'Copydex' or 'Gu')
Plastic padding, braid or velvet ribbon
Compass
Gold paint (Liquid Leaf in 'Renaissance' or 'Classic' gold shades)
Paint brush, pencils, scissors
Pressed flowers
8in diameter circle of baize, felt or 'Fablon' felt (for finishing the mat base when hardboard is used.)

Diagram 64 Table-mats
a. Table-mat with a gold painted border
b. Table-mat edged with gold painted plastic padding. (When using the 'padding' follow instructions for mixing it and apply with a small knife. Dry and sandpaper smooth and apply second thin coat leaving small 'knobbles'. Paint when dry with 'Liquid Leaf' gold paint.)

Work on a clean soft surface and make sure that everything is free of dust and finger marks. Cover the hardboard or cork with a very thin layer of adhesive, and lay the felt on top. Make sure that the edges are flush and that there are no wrinkles in the felt – use a very cool iron to smooth it out if necessary.

Use the compass to mark off the centre of the mat. Using this point as your design centre make a pressed flower arrangement on the felt and follow the 'fixed' method to secure the flowers. It is essential that outside points of the design are equidistant from the edges of the mat. (When perspex is used take extra care to stick the flowers down firmly, otherwise static electricity inherent in such man-made materials will lift the petals and folding will result.)

Run a thin line of adhesive around the edge of the felt and then place the circle of glass or perspex carefully down on top of the flowers and again ensure that the edges are flush with each other. Leave to dry under a weight.

Ornament the edge of the mat with braid or perhaps with a 'knobbly' border of plastic padding painted gold. A fine border of gold paint round the top edge of the glass can be a very pretty alternative (you will need a steady hand for this) with a narrow velvet ribbon to hide the two joins on the side.

When using a hardboard base the mat can be finished off well by the addition of a circular piece of baize or felt underneath. 'Fablon' felt is especially simple to use. 'Picture' weight glass is surprisingly tough and will stand most hot plates; heavy-duty or plate glass can be very heavy and unattractively thick if it is used for table-mats.

Vases Traditional 'posy'-like designs can look very well indeed if they are given a 'vase' or a 'basket' to blossom from. These base shapes can be made from large petals, or leaves cut to shape or trimmed and overlapped to form the required shape. Mosses, lichens, and even thin cross-sections of the common bath loofah can look very attractive and convincing when shaped into a modest vase and arranged beneath the drooping flowers. They also have the added practical advantage that they cover any unwanted and protruding stalks.

Wadding Wadding can easily be found in the haberdashery departments of big stores and also in fabric shops. It is bought by the yard and is usually white or cream in colour. Wadding can be made of cotton or of terylene; the former is softer and easier to use than the 'man-made' varieties, but the extra spring and bounce of the latter is essential when you are making a picture ('free' method) in conjunction with a mount. Wadding can usually be split in half before using in a background – always iron it with a cool iron before using.

Wild Flowers There are many hundreds of common wild flowers in the British Isles, and although a great number will press very well indeed there are, sadly, many others which are not worth the attempt. We have listed only the plants which in our experience press well enough to yield up material that can be easily used in pressed flower designs (diagram 65).

Size, shape and succulence of wild flowers and their leaves are the overriding factors in successful pressing. Sometimes it is size alone

Diagram 65 Wild flowers
a. Rosaceae
b. Violaceae
c. Geraniaceae
d. Hypericaceae
e. Compositae
f. Campanulaceae
g. Umbelliferae
h. Ranunculaceae
i. Boraginaceae

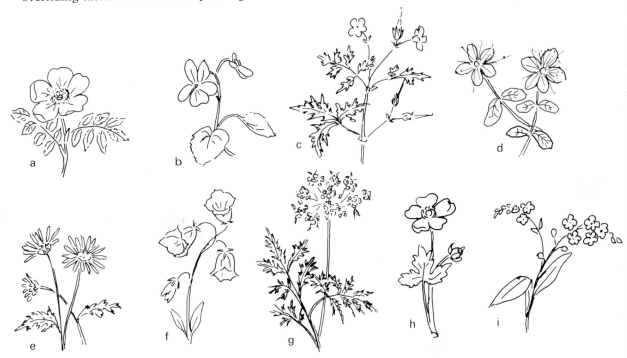

which makes a flower unlikely to fit ultimately into a picture. Irises, foxgloves, thistles, water-lilies are examples of very large flowers.

The shape of a flower – however modest its size – can spoil its chances in your press. In a member of the papilionaceae (the pea) family, the corolla, consisting of standard, keel and two wings which curve protectively over style and stigma, is a three-dimensional exquisite, but laid full-face between blotting paper the wings will invariably become incorrectly folded and the whole shape crushed. Pick half-opened flowers and lay them in profile. Some members of this family, such as melilot, whose florets are narrow, will present little problem.

The family of labiatae – the dead-nettle family – are also unrewarding to press on account of their awkward shape, as are the yellow rattle and the toadflax, which belong to the scrophulariaceae group.

The extensive family of cruciferae present different problems because the petals are very long and are attached only at the base of the deep calyx. When you place these flowers 'full face' on to the paper, you will be tempted to trim away the back, but this will inevitably cause the flower to fall to pieces. This is the cabbage family of vegetable fame, with well-known garden cousins in wallflowers and stocks, and a glance at any member of this common group of flowers will show you the problem. Press flowers in profile or else press each petal seperately and reassemble when dry.

Very small and fragile flowers like the speedwells, ivy-leafed toadflax and the cinquefoils are easily damaged when they are being pressed and will need gentle handling when dry. Very small heads of tufted flowers such as wild mint and clovers can be well worth pressing. Scabious, thrift and other thick flowers can be a little nondescript when they are pressed unless they are very small heads.

The third and final factor which debars a small group of plants is their excessive succulence. This will exclude an old favourite, the bluebell. Orchids, broom-rape and dodder are also full of moisture, and once this soaks into the blotting paper there will be little left of the original colourful flower. Leave these – often rather rare – plants to bloom undisturbed.

Diagram 66 Wild flower shapes

The easiest flowers to press are the star-shaped and open-faced ones (diagram 66). Picked with little or no stem behind the corolla and laid flat on to the blotting paper they will present few problems. Placed sideways or in bud, they will still emerge from the press retaining their charm and beauty and will be instantly recognisable. Celandines, buttercups, wild pansies and dog roses, chamomiles and the delicate florets of the umbellifereae family will be simple to press and quick to dry. Even when the florets are very small and clustered on a single stem, as in the case of the forget-me-not or meadowsweet, they will still press successfully. Wild flowers can be used in designs by themselves or mixed in with garden varieties. A picture made from small humble wild flowers gathered on holiday can be a most happy reminder of family outings, and this can be particularly rewarding when you have been staying in a foreign country. (Check with local people before you pick wild flowers abroad; some countries have protective laws which govern their collection.)

TREES AND CREEPERS WHICH HAVE LEAVES THAT PRESS WELL

Trees

apple	*Malus* bf
common lime	*Tilia vulgaris* bfsl
copper beech	*Fagus sylvatica* fl
crab apple	*Malus sylvestris* bfl
elder	*Sambucus nigra* bf
English oak	*Quercus robur* l
ginkgo	*Ginkgo biloba* l
hawthorn (May)	*Crataegus monogyna* fl
hornbeam	*Carpinus betulus* f
Japanese larch	*Larix kaempferi* l
mountain ash	*Sorbus ancuparia* f
sumach	*Rhus typhina* l
tamarisk	*Tamarix gallica* l
willow	*Salix alba* l

Creepers

clematis	polygonum
ivy	traveller's joy
honeysuckle	vine
jasmine	Virginia creeper
mock vine	white bryony
passion flower	

GLOSSARY OF BOTANICAL TERMS

See also diagram 68

Anther The end of the stamen holding the pollen.

Biennial A plant that takes two years to complete its life cycle.

Bract A small unformed leaf near the flower head or at the base of the flower stalk.

Calyx The outermost whorl of the perianth. The leaf-like covering which encloses a bud and which lies at the back of the flower.

Corymb A flat-topped cluster of flowers, the stalks of which arise one above the other from the stem.

Family A group of related plants.

Floret A small flower which is part of a cluster.

Frond A small leaf-like part of a fern.

Genus The smallest natural group containing related but distinct species.

Glaucous Covered with greenish-blue bloom.

Hirsute Hairy (usually soft).

Perennial A flower that lives for more than two years and usually flowers annually.

Perianth A complete floral envelope of petals and sepals.

Sepal A leaf of the calyx.

Species The basic unit of classification of plants.

Spur A slender projection at the back of the flower (sometimes hook-shaped).

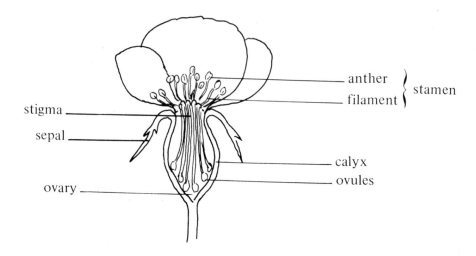

Stamen One of the small delicate spikes lying in the centre of the flower (usually in a ring), carrying pollen at the top in the anther. Male reproductive organ.

Succulent Juicy.

Variety A distinct form of a plant.

BOTANICAL CLASSIFICATION

International botanical classification is by family, genus, species and variety. The variety (if any) is shown in quotation marks.

English Name	Family	Genus	Species
snowdrop	amaryllidaceae	Galanthus	nivalis
herb Robert	geraniaceae	Geranium	robertianum

BIBLIOGRAPHY

Garden flowers

Hay, Roy and Synge, Patrick M., *Dictionary of Garden Plants in Colour*, Micheal Joseph and Ebury Press (in collaboration with the Royal Horticultural Society), London, 1969

Anderson, E.B., etc., *Oxford Book of Garden Flowers*, Oxford University Press, Oxford, 1964

Wild Flowers

Martin W. Keble, *Concise British Flora in Colour*, Michael Joseph and Ebury Press, London, 1965

Fitter, Alistair and Richard, *Wild Flowers of Britain and Northern Europe*, Collins, London, 1974

Phillips, Roger, *Wild Flowers of Britain*, Pan Books and Ward Lock, London, 1977

Ferns

Phillips, Roger, *Grasses, Ferns, Mosses and Lichens of Great Britain and Ireland*, Pan Books, London, 1980

Houseplants

Hessayon, Dr. D.G. & J.P., *Be your own Houseplant Spotter*, Pan Britannica Industries, 1977

Framing Pictures

Woods, Michael, *Mounting and Framing Pictures*, Batsford, London, 1981

LIST OF SUPPLIERS

Garden centres and nurserymen
Notcutts Nurseries Ltd (Ipswich) and branches.

Ferns, 'foliage' plants and houseplants
Thomas Rochford and Son, Turnford, Hertfordshire.

Frame makers and 'heat-sealing' specialists
Arthur Harding, The Old Bakery, High Cross, Nr. Ware, Hertfordshire. Deben Gallery, Woodbridge, Suffolk.

Greeting cards and calendars for pressed flower decoration
Impress Cards, Slough Farm, Westhall, Halesworth, Suffolk
Paperchase, Tottenham Court Road, London.

Index

(numbers in *italics* refer to diagram or figure numbers)